WHAT OTHERS ARE SAYING ABOUT THIS BOOK

*For the past twenty-five years I have worked in the court system, making legal decisions that determined the consequences of the wrong choices made by others. Too often, those decisions did little to effectively deal with the underlying problems of drug and alcohol abuse, and of anger and bitterness, that so heavily contributed to most of the wrong choices that were made. In **FATHER WOUNDS**, Bob Reccord shares a problem-solving strategy that will be more effective and will help to heal our communities, one wounded person at a time, one right choice at a time.*

The Honorable Randy T. Rogers

*After eleven years in the talk radio business—and hosting over two thousand shows—one thing that men do NOT like to talk about is the damage that was done to them by their fathers. Most of my closest friends have dealt with "Father Wounds" for years, and for their sake (and countless others), I thank God that my friend Bob Reccord continues to minister to these men and especially through his book **ENDING THE CYCLE OF FATHER WOUNDS**. Bob not only deals with the issues of the past to find forgiveness and healing, but the incredible wisdom he shares will also help fathers make sure they don't repeat the wounding with their own children. Every man in America with Father Wounds needs to read and receive the healing and hope this book offers.*

Steve Noble, Host
The Steve Noble Radio Show

Bob Reccord is an expert in many things, but he excels when it comes to relationships! Unfortunately, relationships are imperfect; we all become wounded at some point. Tragically if we do not learn to heal from our hurts, then we will bleed on other people who never even cut us. Bob gives a process to help people deal with wounds that sometimes come from having imperfect earthly fathers. In speaking to tens of thousands of men, Bob has shared his own personal journey in creating a road map for others to heal through a relationship with a perfect heavenly Father. This book will not only bless you; it will transform you!

Dr. Dwight "Ike" Reighard
Senior Pastor, Piedmont
Baptist Church, Marietta,
Georgia
Co-Author with Zig Ziglar

*It's the heartbreaking epidemic of this generation—and more people deal with it on a daily basis than we can possibly imagine. Fatherlessness—whether physical or emotional—is the open wound that only the grace of God can heal. I rejoice at this outstanding resource Bob Reccord has given us. **FATHER WOUNDS** has such rich content! May God's love as the only perfect Father wash over you in a real and personal way, and may it stay with you forever as this book helps heal those wounds in you or someone you love.*

Dr. Jeremy Morton
Senior Pastor, Woodstock
Baptist Church, Woodstock,
Georgia

How impactful is ENDING THE CYCLE OF FATHER WOUNDS? In early 2019 I took a dozen men to a men's conference where Bob spoke on this subject. I later asked those men to share their experiences of Bob's message with a much larger group of approximately one hundred men. A quiet pensiveness pervaded the room, as untold tears bore witness to wounds long buried—now ushered into the light and desperate for healing. This effect from a message heard secondhand? YES! So steel yourself for an unparalleled impact upon not only your own life but the lives of those closest to you as well.

Jeff Boswell
Managing Anesthesiologist
Anesthesia Department at Aiken,
S.C. Regional Medical Centers

FATHER WOUNDS is a book that should be read by every father, grandfather, and adult son, regardless of their faith. Bob Reccord peels back the wounds that every boy, man, and daughter has experienced. Best of all, he offers healing solutions that only God can bring.

Terry Van Someren
Publisher of *The Complete Biblical Library*

For both culture and churches, there is no more important topic to discuss than the importance of a godly and engaged father to his children. Bob Reccord and Rick Fowler have hit the bull's-eye blending the biblical narrative of fatherhood with the daily challenge of practical application. In the relativistic age in which we live, such rare works are a must for the leaders of the home!

Dr. Emir Caner
President
Truett McConnell University

*As a boy raised by a single mom, my question is twofold: What did I miss and how will I learn what I missed? **FATHER WOUNDS** will be an incredible help with my past and a better help as to how I should father. What a gift!*

Dr. Johnny Hunt
Former President of Southern
Baptist Convention
33 years Senior Pastor of
First Baptist Woodstock,
Georgia

Rather than avoid sensitive and difficult "Father Wound" issues, Bob Reccord addresses them head-on in a biblical, healthy way. Every male is born to be a warrior, but so many are wounded growing up by loss of their father through death, divorce, distance, or dysfunction. Bob not only addresses the heart of the wound but reveals the heart of the Healer. Get ready to embrace your wound, forgive, seek your true Father's healing, and trust His call to true manhood.

I would highly recommend this great, biblical, God-centered book for men who have been wounded by their earthly fathers. This book will help them embrace the pain, forgive, and see God as their perfect heavenly Father!

Art Remington Jr.
National Ambassador-At-Large
for Promise Keepers
Pastor

The roles of a father and of a mother are the most important God-given assignments in the world. But fathers are often left without help or encouragement. Assistance, guidance, and encouragement have just arrived with this wonderful book from Bob Reccord. What strengthens its message is that it is written by one of the finest dads I have ever known or met. Read, benefit, be challenged and blessed!

Dr. Phil Roberts
Former President
Midwestern Baptist Theological
Seminary

I am confident that the readers of **ENDING THE CYCLE OF FATHER WOUNDS** *will find encouragement, support, and a "traveling companion of sort" as they move toward healing. It's a book that should be on the shelf of every man and woman!*

Steve Fischer
Pastoral Care Ministries
Stonebriar Community Church
Frisco, Texas
(Dr. Chuck Swindoll, Sr. Pastor)

Some of the most devastating and destructive wounds are those that aren't so obvious or easily observed. This fact is undoubtedly true for the wounds suffered from fathers—who are often wounded themselves. In **FATHER WOUNDS**, *my friend Bob Reccord not only identifies the problem but traces the root cause and presents a way to heal the hurt and stop the cycle of the wounded causing more wounds in the lives of those they love the most. I'm personally thankful for this timely and insightful book and pray that it helps us as fathers to end the cycle that is hurting so many families and fathers today.*

Brad Whitt
Senior Pastor
Abilene Baptist Church
Augusta, Georgia

The impact of a father on the lives of his children is profound—for good or bad. When things go wrong, help is needed. This book is that help! **FATHER WOUNDS** *is prescriptive—addressing the fallout of dysfunctional fathering and offering help for those dealing with Father Wounds. In addition,* **FATHER WOUNDS** *is preventative—offering useful guidelines for those who want to "break the cycle" of dysfunction and develop healthy parenting skills. Highly recommended!*

Dr. Joe Cook
Graduate Professor of
Professional Counseling
Dallas Baptist University

One of the most important relationships for any man is with his father. Through that relationship a son learns self-worth, character, work ethic, responsibility—how to be a man. Sadly, most fathers were never taught how to love, lead, and mentor their sons. Because of that, most sons feel to some degree estranged from their fathers and unequipped to lead their families. Therefore, a destructive cycle continues from generation to generation. In his book **FATHER WOUNDS**, *Bob Reccord provides insights that will help every man discover and deal with strained and ruptured issues in his relationship with his father, his stepdad, or the father figure in his life. Dr. Reccord also teaches how to end the destructive cycle and chart a new course filled with healthy, loving relationships.* **FATHER WOUNDS** *is a must-read for every man (and woman) who desires to build a legacy through his (or her) children.*

Dr. Thomas Hammond
Exec. Director, Georgia Baptist
Convention

Bob Reccord has powerfully addressed one of the most important issues facing our world today! **FATHER WOUNDS** *reminds us that we live among "the walking wounded," and much of that has been caused by "friendly fire." In this very practical guide, Bob helps us identify the dangers of Father Wounds, provides us with great personal insight and healing answers, and gives us great hope for the future of transformed relationships. As you read you will not only find yourself, but you will find the direction you need rooted in biblical principle. No matter what your family background, this is a must-read for all of us. When you have read it, you'll be sharing it with someone else!*

Dr. Mike Hamlet
Sr. Pastor, First Baptist
North Spartanburg, South Carolina

*Bob Reccord has written **FATHER WOUNDS** out of extensive experience in his own life and his deep involvement in ministry to many thousands of men across our nation. In this book, he puts us in touch with our own "Father Wounds" and how those wounds limit the strength of our lives and families.*

He is a man's man. He brings together the priority and wisdom of Scripture and the healing power of God's grace and God's Word.

Bob Reccord is real. He is transparent. He provides practical steps for our continued healing.

Thank you, Bob Reccord, for your integrity and your wisdom in this labor of love to bless our lives and families.

> Dr. Jerry Kirk
> Former Pastor, College
> Hill Presbyterian Church,
> Cincinnati, Ohio
> Founder, The Prayer Covenant
> Movement

ENDING THE CYCLE OF

FATHER WOUNDS

*Hope for Healing, and
Preventing Infections
Caused by Relational
Wounds*

BOB RECCORD
With Dr. Rick Fowler

Ending the Cycle of Father Wounds: Hope for Healing and Preventing Infections Caused by Relational Wounds

Copyright ©January 2020 by Bob Reccord

Published by M & R Legacy Publishing
Total Life Impact Ministries
Canton, Georgia

ISBN for print book   978-0-9980479-2-8

ISBN for eBook   978-0-9980479-3-5

Dedication

To my biological mother and father: I thank them for giving me life.

To my adoptive mother and father: I thank them for giving me a chance to live that life well.

To my wonderful wife of forty-seven years, Cheryl, who has patiently walked beside me through these years and has loved and supported me through what I have learned, and who has been a great help and support as I have grown, overcome, and become a better man, husband, father and, now, grandfather.

To my grown children—Christy, Bryan, and Ashley—to whom I'm sure I unintentionally gave some Father Wounds because of my own, but who have loved me despite that and from whom I treasure the word Dad. I thank them for helping me grow along the journey, see my mistakes, and, more than once, push a "reset" button relationally.

To many others along the way who personally experienced Father Wounds but who have made a significant contribution and impact upon my life, including the following:

    Dr. Leighton Ford

    Steve Puckett

    Dr. Jay Strack

    Dr. Jim Daly

    Pat MacMillan

    And numerous others—too many to be named

To George Williams, who encouraged me repeatedly to do this book and has been a wonderful friend for so many years.

To Dr. Johnny Hunt, who granted me the venue at his fabulous men's conference to address this issue to thousands of men in 2019.

To Helen Spore, who worked her magic in editing.

To Terry Van Someren, who created the cover for this book but first read the manuscript in its entirety to help get the right feel and message conveyed in what people see.

To the Peachtree Publishing Services team, who were a great help, again, in finalizing the book for print to hopefully help many lives and relationships heal and prevent relational damage in the nerve center of society—the home.

Table of Contents

XV   FOREWORD

XVII   A WORD OF INTRODUCTION

I   CHAPTER I
           Fathers Rock!

8   CHAPTER 2
           Wounded Warriors

16   CHAPTER 3
           Taking a Personal Examination

24   CHAPTER 4
           Why So Many Wounded, and Why So Many Wounds?

36   CHAPTER 5
           Fathers in Search of Solidity and Significance

43   CHAPTER 6
           What Every Child Needs in a Dad

59   CHAPTER 7
           A Word from the Front-Row Seats

70   CHAPTER 8
           Every Rupture Needs to Be Restored

76   CHAPTER 9
           The Miracle of Forgiveness

88   CHAPTER 10
God States His Expectation

96   CHAPTER 11
"What Do You Mean Honor Your Father? He Doesn't
Deserve it!"

105   CHAPTER 12
Choosing to Recover—The Pathway to Peace

123   CHAPTER 13
Key Steps to Finding Closure

135   CHAPTER 14
The Choice Is Yours!

148   APPENDIX

Foreword

...it has been said that paternity is a career imposed on you one fine morning without any inquiry as to your fitness for it. That is why there are so many fathers who have children, but so few children who have fathers.

Adlai Stevenson[1]

With the banging of divorce court gavels so loud we can no longer hear the wedding bells and the crying of the children so deafening because of the failing of the fathers, this book should become required reading for all men of all ages. I do not make that statement often, but this is a book that can truly bring about the healing of the memories and if applied quickly could prevent wounds that may never heal. Though stated years ago, the fact of the statement has exploded over the decades following. As the founder of Student Leadership University, I have the joy of working with thousands of students annually and many of the adults in their lives as well. While doing so, I hear and see a lot. Much of it is incredible—overwhelming talent, bright minds, non-ending potential, life goals and passion. But scattered everywhere in the journey I find both young people and adults who among all the positives, are carrying immense baggage. So much so, I'm tempted to have porters at all of our meetings. Baggage from emotional wounds which have developed into relational "infections" which are adversely affecting not only their one life, but the lives

---

1 Peter S. Seymour, A Father's Love (Kansas City: Hallmark Books, 1972), p. 5.

of those around them…many of whom are family and friends. Sadly, often those wounds come from relationships with their father, step-dad of the father figure in their life. And if they aren't addressed, and ruptured relationships repaired (and hopefully restored), the wounds will likely be passed on through them, often unintentionally, to succeeding generations.

I have known Bob Reccord for over thirty years, and in such a time span you get to know that person well, both their strengths and weaknesses, their victories and defeats, and their joys as well as their wounds. Like me, Bob experienced Father Wounds not just from one dad, but multiple ones. In his case it was both an alcoholic biological father as well as a wounded adopted dad. Both of us came to the crossroads in our life of determining if we were going to allow ourselves to merely be another "victim" of difficult and wounding upbringing, or if we were going to do whatever it took to become a Victor over the circumstances dealt to us. Would our wounds become stumbling blocks or stepping stones?

In **ENDING THE CYCLE OF FATHER WOUNDS** Bob has masterfully and very vulnerably through his own journey, brought practical, workable and transformational principles and steps to the reader to become an Overcomer as well. But to do so, first a person has to be honest enough to admit where they really are. To help enable that, Bob and Dr. Rick Fowler worked together to offer a self-administered assessment tool in Chapter 3 which will help the reader determine how much Father Wounds most likely influences and affects their life. With a pen in hand you can know in a matter of moments *where you really are!*

To enable anyone to understand key insights of "how we got here" in the area of Father Wounds the book traces some watershed influencers which have led to wounded dads, who too often wound others—whether intentionally, or much more often, unintentionally. It will open the reader's eyes as to some of the cultural impacts which have so negatively rocked today's family structure.

Bob will then, with the assistance of Dr. Rick Fowler, chart a course for anyone who is willing to repair and hopefully restore ruptured relationships with their dad, step-dad or an important father figure in their journey. The journey will be simple...but often not easy. It will be both a destination, and a journey. But once taken, and fulfilled, it will be a GAME CHANGER!

I invite you, along with Bob and Rick, to journey with us. Come along and discover some of the things we have found along the rocky, challenging authentic road to healing Father Wounds... and even more importantly, in preventing Father Wounds in the future. Trust me; this is a journey you will be glad you took—not only for your sake, but for the sake of all those around you!

Dr. Jay Strack
Founder, Student Leadership
University
www.Slulead.com

A Word of Introduction

Have you ever noticed that as bad as physical wounds of different types can be, it is often the resulting infections that can cause significant short-range complications and dangers, not to mention long-term and lasting implications?

So it is with relational wounds. The wounds themselves are bad enough when experienced, but the infections that develop over time, through neglect or even by denial, can be devastating and crippling. The worst wounds come from those closest to us, such as immediate family. In the environment where every child rightly expects safety and security, wounds from "friendly fire" can be crippling and devastating.

But why is it that the infections resulting from wounds can do so much damage?

The history of medical science gives us some insight into the answer. For long seasons of history the mortality rates of various types of medical procedures were astronomical. Surgery was seen as only a last resort when there was no other choice. Relatively simple procedures such as child birth saw high death rates. And the question that haunted the medical field was *Why*?

Looking backward in history we now know that doctors and medical personnel had not discovered the deadly cause—germs. They couldn't be seen. They weren't evident. But they were deadly.

Doctors had long simply cleaned scalpels and wiped them on a rag, a bloody smock, or whatever was handy, and then put it to use again in the next medical procedure. At times as many as half the patients died.

Thankfully, a medical pioneer arose and turned the tide, which benefited us all and changed the course of history. In 1847 Ignaz Semmelweis discovered that making doctors wash their hands and scrub and clean their fingernails dramatically cut the death rate in maternity wards as well as in other surgeries. Yet, despite the "proof being in the pudding" of significant rises in survival rates, his own colleagues fought against him and his procedures. While he would battle for more sterile environments all his life, he would die without seeing these relatively simple safety procedures accepted and widely practiced in medicine!

Why? What was the holdup?

Germs were invisible, not seen with the naked eye. Sterilization procedures went against the grain of "the way we've always done it." People often don't like the inconvenience of change, even when the results are health and healing, and thus continue on in their dysfunction.

Finally in 1862, French chemist and microbiologist Louis Pasteur stepped onto the scientific scene and discovered micro-organisms (germs) under the microscope. Those invisible germs were found to cause disease and infections. That led to break-throughs in understanding the answers to the why questions and increasingly led to much-needed steps of safety and recov-ery in the medical arenas. In 1867 an English physician greatly reduced the mortality rate of his patients by using a carbolic spray solution as he operated, spraying it in the wound, on the articles in contact with the wound, and on the hands of the op-erating team. Slowly, the needed change was finally making sense. (This will be important to keep in mind as you read the story of the shooting of President William McKinley in chap-ter 9. If only changes would have occurred faster, which would have greatly helped in reducing infections that had such a tragic impact when he was shot in 1901!)

Even so, changes and admissions of wrong or inadequate processes and procedures—or adapting better and healthier actions and steps—often come slowly. People most often prefer to hold positions such as "But we've always done it this way," "Things will be fine; we just need to leave it alone," "It will work out with time," or "Somebody else caused this, not me!"

This book not only addresses the issue of Father Wounds (which I have found perhaps the majority of both men and women experience) but also acknowledges the fact that often they occur in a cycle within a family culture. One generation after the other can carry on the tendency to inflict them either intentionally or, perhaps more often, unintentionally. And the initial wound (by an action or inaction) is most often complicated and exacerbated by unseen *infections* such as resentment, anger, bitterness, and lack of forgiveness.

Through the years hundreds have shared their stories with me of how such wounds have infected and affected not only their personal lives but also the lives of their own families, which they would later establish through marriages of their own.

Thus, the questions come:

- What is a Father Wound?
- Why and how do they occur?
- If they often occur in family cycles, how do you stop them?
- How can you repair them?
- How, even more proactively, can you prevent them?

This book addresses those questions head-on. It doesn't tiptoe through the tulips of "easy answers." Rather, it speaks directly and vulnerably to these critical questions.

I have brought my great friend Dr. Rick Fowler into the writing project to add the voice of one of the most respected counselors and coaches I know. He brings the experience of over 35,000 counseling sessions with individuals of all races, backgrounds, ages, and gender—many of whom were the recipients of Father Wounds. I have over forty years of leadership and ministry experience and have personally experienced Father Wounds in my own life.

We want this book to help you repair the impact of any Father Wounds you may have experienced, and to help prevent future Father Wounds from occurring. As you read it, I invite you to read it from two perspectives:

1. Evaluate honestly and vulnerably your own relationship with your father, stepfather, or father figure.

2. If you are a dad, granddad, or key father figure in someone's life, evaluate yourself to determine if you have possibly inflicted Father Wounds, either intentionally or unintentionally, or if you may be in danger of doing so.

Both of these are important not only for you but also for those closest and dearest to you. And an honest, straightforward addressing of these two areas could make all the difference for a life-changing future—both for you and those you love.

Bob Reccord
January 2020

| Fathers Rock!

THERE IS NO such thing as a perfect parent—or a guaranteed perfect outcome of parenting, for that matter.

God the Father would be the one exception of "perfect parent." But, take a pause and reflect on the challenge He experienced with His first two "children," Adam and Eve!

Let's face it: good parenting isn't easy! And it surely is not just a destination; it truly is a journey. In this "instant" society driven by microprocessors, digital data, and voice-activated artificial intelligence, it is tempting to expect parenting to happen in *3 easy steps* or by *5 key principles*. But it just isn't that easy—or fast.

You've probably heard it said that "the hand that rocks the cradle rules the world." And who would argue with that?

But equally important are fathers. While any male can become a father through a biological act, it requires intentional focus, devotion, and tons of work to be a *good* one! And it takes a lifetime.

Fathers can build adequacy and security in their kids—or leave voids and wounds, as their children become collateral damage.

Research clearly shows that where a father is physically and emotionally engaged, children are by far healthier, stronger emotionally, more secure socially and relationally, and happier. And as for fathers, it has well been pointed out that one of the most important things a father can do for his children is to love their mother visibly and daily in front of the kids. This provides a secure and pleasant environment where development can happen in the manner that God intended.

Add to that, when there is a strong marriage in the home, children have a significantly increased probability of maturing in a healthy and well-adjusted manner. These children will also have a far greater chance of having emotionally healthy and solidly secure marriages and families of their own, having benefited from a good model.

But just look around. Read a paper from the newsstand or check your favorite digital device. In your vehicle listen to the news on your radio as you travel, or tune in to the news via your TV at home. Take it one step further and watch a session or two of *Dr. Phil.* It doesn't take but a cursory focus to acknowledge that families are on shaky ground with breakdown fractures running throughout the base of many. And often, tragically, it has to do with the absence—emotionally and/or physically—of dads.

THE HIGH NEED FOR PRESENT, ENGAGED DADS

"Whether you're a father, grandfather or a father figure, you have a tremendous influence and power—probably more than you realize. You have the power to strengthen the next generation . . . or destroy it. Your invisible presence will be felt for decades."[2] What profound words from Dr. Ken Canfield who founded The National Center of Fathering! Kids are not simply a biological reality; *they are a trust.* And every father has a stewardship of that trust for which he will be held responsible.

---

2   Ken Canfield, *They Call Me Dad* (West Monroe, Louisiana: Howard Publishing, 2005), p 175.

Research shows that when fathers are present and engaged in their kids' lives, the impact is both tangible and very significant! The National Center for Fathering reveals that studies show the following:

- Preschoolers with present/engaged fathers develop much stronger verbal skills.
- Children with actively engaged fathers present much fewer behavioral problems at school.
- Highly engaged fathers significantly contribute to children's increased mental dexterity, empathy, and self-control.
- Such children are at greatly decreased risk of alcohol and drug abuse.
- Children with involved fathers have less emotional and behavioral difficulties in adolescence.
- Teenagers who feel close to their fathers in adolescence go on to have more satisfactory adult marital relationships.
- Girls who have a strong relationship with their fathers during adolescence show a lack of psychological distress in adult life.
- When fathers are involved, their children learn more, perform better in school, and exhibit healthier behavior.[3]

On the other hand, where fathers are absent and/or disengaged, the results are as diametrically opposite as possible. Just reverse everything you just read and multiply it!

When it comes to the importance of a dad in a child's life, there is no way to overstate its value.

Even Jesus acknowledged the critical importance of a father. Did you realize that in the Gospel of John, Jesus referred to His heavenly father twenty-five times? And in John 5:19 Jesus

---

3 www.fathers.com

declared, "The Son . . . can do only what he sees his Father doing." He took His cues for living and leading from what He observed in His heavenly father and what He saw Him do.

In John 10:30 Jesus proclaimed, "I and the Father are one," emphasizing the intimacy between the two.

And recall that when Jesus launched His ministry, He traveled to where John the Baptist was attracting great crowds and there requested that John baptize Him. It was at that moment that a dove descended from heaven and a voice from heaven was heard to say, "You are my Son, whom I love; with you I am well pleased" (Mark 1:11).

What a powerful and significant statement! God the Father gave Jesus a strong identity—*my beloved son*; He also gave Him overwhelming affirmation—*in whom I am well pleased*. I love the way the Living Bible (TLB) says it: "You are my beloved Son; you are my Delight." What child would not give everything to hear their father state words like that on a regular basis?

Notice key points and the pattern that God the Father crafted in these words and modeled for earthly dads:

- **He began with extending a treasured identity**—Every child needs to know they are a treasured part of a family. *Belonging* is a key sense in emotional security. What child doesn't swell with pride and bask in security when they hear their dad proclaim, "That's my boy!" or "I'm so proud that she's my daughter!"—especially when these declarations are made based on *the character of the child*, not merely the "performance" of the child.

- **He voiced an affirming blessing**—God pointed out that He was "well pleased" with His Son. He publicly affirmed His Son in front of others. A child will swell with a sense of significance when a blessing comes from their dad, especially

4

when it is public in front of others. A great resource for dads in this area on what a blessing is and how to do it is the book *The Blessing* by Gary Smalley and John Trent.

- **He extended a public commendation**—God encouraged others to "listen to" His Son (Matthew 17:5; Mark 9:7). What a wonderful picture of how a dad holds the power to authenticate a child as a contributor to others, someone who is worth paying attention to and who has words, actions or intentions that will benefit those around him or her.

Our heavenly Father is indeed a model for every earthly dad. In fact, did you realize that kids often form a lot of their view of God from their father? There is an innate need and longing in every person to know the God who created them, and we take many of our early cues in childhood and adolescence from what we observe and experience in our earthly fathers.

ATTENTION DADS!

Dad, you have a critical role. Your presence and engagement are vital! Without your impact there is an inevitable void left.

So, I'll leave you with just a few warm-up encouragements to every dad:

- Since we dads are "fix it" people, there is nothing in life more important to *fix* than our relationships at home.
- It will be critical to keep in mind that the greatest need in every son is to feel *adequate* in his dad's eyes. Conversely, the greatest fear of every son is to feel *inadequate*.
- Likewise, the greatest need of every daughter is to feel loved and *secure*. Her greatest fear will be *insecurity*. Dads play a pivotal role here.

- Every dad will need to define what is *success* and what brings *significance*. And these are most often not the same thing. *Success* is often seen as conquering or accomplishing, while true *significance* is most often found in life's most important relationships and giving oneself away in the service of others.

NOTES

2 Wounded Warriors

E VERY MALE HAS a warrior deep within.
John Eldredge, in his blockbuster book *Wild at Heart*, told us
that every guy has three main needs in his life:

- A battle to fight
- A beauty to rescue
- An adventure to live[4]

Notice the quality listed first.

We as guys grow up playing Cowboys and Indians, army, and
games like dodgeball. Our focus is to *win*—to conquer. Most often we thrive on competition. And we love sports with bodily
contact!

Often, we can't even approach a board game without an overwhelming drive to come out on top. Losing is *not* an option.

Let's admit it: females love the Hallmark Channel, Lifetime,
and what is often referred to as "chick flicks." Someone has said
that the typical plot of these "flicks" is sophisticated girl from big

---

4 John Eldredge, *Wild at Heart* (Nashville, Tennessee: Thomas Nelson
   Publishers, 2001).

city experiences a trauma, runs away to small town, meets local everyday guy, after much internal conflict falls in love, and struggles with justifying how life can be so simple. Throw in a dog, and you've got a real winner. And when it comes to movies, titles such as *Sweet Home Alabama, A Walk to Remember, While You Were Sleeping,* and *Sleepless in Seattle* quickly bubble to the surface and bring dreamy smiles to the faces of most females.

But for a guy, give them *Gettysburg, Patton, Die Hard, Band of Brothers, Braveheart, Hoosiers,* and *Rudy.*

Unfortunately, somewhere along the way, too often young warriors are wounded on the battlefield of growing up. And far too often the wounds come from "friendly fire."

Friendly fire can be unintended—yet so tragic.

When a robbery alarm came in to the 102nd Precinct from a T-Mobile store close to Kennedy International Airport in New York City, forty-two-year-old detective Brian Simonsen responded. He wasn't even on active duty but volunteered to go with a fellow sergeant.

As the men entered the store, they saw a man approaching them pointing what appeared to be a handgun in their direction. Opening fire, they quickly retreated out of the store. Other officers had arrived in the meantime, and in the ensuing confusion, they also opened fire.

Moments later Officer Brian Simonsen lay dead. Killed by friendly fire. The sergeant with him was wounded as well.

No one meant it to happen.

It wasn't intentional.

If they could have done it over again, it would have gone down totally differently.

But the facts are the facts.

It often happens like that in families as well. Often no one actually means for "wounds" to happen. The intention is not to

9

leave someone critically hurt. But things happen fast. Mouths are in motion before minds are in gear. Words fly—and wound—like gunfire.

Or at a critical moment when a dad is desperately needed to be present, he is absent. Sometimes physically. Other times emotionally. But absent, nonetheless.

Isn't it unnerving how a dad can even be physically present but emotionally absent all at the same time?

And the result: inevitably serious "wounds" by friendly fire.

. . . .

WOUNDS THAT DON'T GO AWAY

So what exactly is a Father Wound, you ask?

Great question. Important question.

Over the last twenty-five years I have had a passion for speaking to men. Over just a bit more than a decade I have been honored to address some 275,000 men. Many have told me their stories. And many have been the victims of Father Wounds.

I often ask a simple question:

> *How many of you had a dad, stepdad, or father figure who regularly and consistently told you he loved you unconditionally and was proud of you for who you were, not just for how you performed, and was regularly engaged with you and those things important to you as you were growing up?*

Sadly, almost without exception, no more than 20 to 25 percent of the men present respond in the affirmative. Stop and let it sink in how many do not respond positively!

So what is a Father Wound?

First, let's look at the definition of *wound*.

The Merriam-Webster Dictionary *defines* wound *as "an injury to the body (as from violence, accident, or surgery) that typically involves laceration or breaking of a membrane (such as the skin) and usually damage to underlying tissues."* [5]

Now, use that definition and move it into the realm of relationships, especially that of a dad and a child. Perhaps it would sound something like this:

An injury to the heart and soul (whether by words, actions or inactions) that typically involves damage to, or breaking, of a relationship

Let's take it one step further and establish a working definition of a Father Wound:

An emotional injury to the heart and soul caused by what a dad, stepdad, or father figure did—or did not do—in words, actions, or inactions as a child grew through childhood and adolescence, damaging or rupturing relationships as a result.

It requires healing and, if left unattended, will become deeper and more "infected." Following proper cleansing and treatment, it will require time to heal.

So many of us, deep down inside, have a void and father pain because we never felt embraced, accepted, and affirmed by our father (stepfather, or father figure) in the manner that we needed to be.

---

5   *Merriam-Webster*, s.v. "wound (n.)," accessed December 17, 2019, http://www.merriam-webster.com/dictionary/wound.

A FEW KEY FACTS REGARDING FATHER WOUNDS

As a historically well-known TV detective used to say, we stand in need of "just the facts." Here are a few facts regarding Father Wounds:

- They tend to be multigenerational—the affect tends to go on and on.
- Wounded men wound others—often unintentionally.
- They are caused by inaction as often as action.
- Due to the male makeup and "wiring," the attempt is often to ignore them or pretend they do not exist.
- Wounds heal slowly and depend on proper care and action.

In view of the fact that Father Wounds really exist, and in big numbers, it needs to be quickly and firmly said that this in no way makes a villain of fathers. It simply points out that all of us have clay feet. All of us make mistakes. Men, in many ways, find themselves on a tough uphill trek by being raised in a culture that too often declares hollow but influential guidelines for males, such as the following:

- Big boys don't cry!
- Suck it up!
- No pain, no gain!
- Don't show your emotions!
- Never look weak!

Maybe it's a wonder we fathers don't cause more challenges than we do.

So, having pointed this out, the purpose of this book is not to put down anyone but rather to encourage every man that *it is not too late to turn corners, repair damage, heal wounds, and move into a great, promise-filled future.*

But it will take acknowledging some issues, making some potentially tough decisions, and taking some intentional action steps for the future. And any guy can do it!

In collecting information from hundreds and hundreds of men, let me share with you the results of what men themselves have said are the source(s) of their Father Wounds. As you can imagine, many men said the wounds resulted from more than just one sole cause. As they have looked deep within their souls, they have discovered the Wounds have come from a dad, stepdad, granddad, or father figure who did the following:

- Abused drugs or alcohol   6%
- Wasn't engaged, even when home   66%
- Was abusive physically, emotionally, or verbally   20%
- Failed to regularly express love and pride   58%
- Manipulated and was overcontrolling   10%
- Did not set boundaries; was too lenient   9%
- Lived hypocritically and inconsistently   8.5%
  (walk didn't match talk, public and private life varied)
- Played favorites with kids in home   9%
- Continually criticized and put down   14%
- Was abusive to mother or unfaithful to her   14%
- Never taught or modeled how to become a
  godly man   19%
- Wasn't there for major events that were
  important to child   41%
- Made fun of child's faith, belief in Christ   2%
- Abandoned child without explanation   4%

Just think, we guys often walk into marriage, fatherhood, jobs, churches, and even grandfathering with these wounds unattended. No wonder we can have so many unexpected challenges!

Before we end this chapter, would you join me in acknowledging that we guys often don't have it all together? And that we have often been wounded in our own past and, without meaning to, can carry the wounds into the present, often unintentionally?

If we can man up with an admission like that, we are well positioned to move forward toward great days by finishing the journey through which this book will take us.

NOTES

3 Taking a Personal Examination

With so many having been impacted by Father Wounds, you may know for a fact that you were in the fortunate minority that was not affected. Take some time and thank God for your upbringing, as well as for your father, stepfather, or father figure, and that you didn't have to go through the hurt and disappointment that would have been the result. You were blessed with a running start on healthy living and relationships.

On the other hand, you may have no doubt about the reality of Father Wounds because you have experienced them firsthand. You saw yourself in some of the answers of the previous chapters. You have personally experienced one or more of the numerous causes for damage to your heart and soul as you were growing up. If so, I'm so sorry. I wish I could snap a finger to heal and restore it all without your having to work through anything. But, unfortunately, I can't. This book is for you! Keep reading, as it was created to help you successfully get to healing, restoration, and wholeness.

But perhaps you have questions. You aren't quite sure whether the issue applies to you. In some ways, you feel it does—and in other ways, you're not quite sure. So, is there a way to do a check-up and see, like going to a doctor to check on your physical health? Is there an examination that can detect an indication of what does, or does not, affect you?

Allow me to introduce you to a good friend of mine who has agreed to contribute a helping hand to this as a counseling professional. Dr. Rick Fowler is a licensed Christian therapist who has been a professor of counseling at four universities and is presently a full professor at Truett-McConnell University in Georgia. During his journey, he has also coached basketball and served as a sports therapist to athletic teams, as he does presently. As great as all that is, what amazes me most is that he has participated in over 35,000 counseling sessions in which he has helped others work through the issues of their lives. That's equivalent to four years of counseling if it were done twenty-four hours per day, seven days a week!

Rick has created a self-administered assessment tool to help you determine if Father Wounds are a factor in your journey. So grab a pen and work through the assessment, which you can self-measure when you are finished. Be honest. Put "rose-colored glasses" aside. Be realistic. I hope you find it helpful.

FATHER WOUND ASSESSMENT

Directions: Each question begins with "As I grew up, my dad ..." Beside each statement, put a

"4" if the statement is 85–100% accurate

"3" if the statement is 64–84% accurate

"2" if the statement is 37–63% accurate

"1" if the statement is 16–36% accurate

"0" if the statement is 0–15% accurate

Note: When answering these questions, you may want to complete this assessment two times if you also lived with a stepfather (one assessment on biological dad; the second, on stepdad).

As I grew up, my dad ...

1. _____ would do some activity with me, alone, at least one time a week.

2. _____ never used "foul" language when talking to me.

3. _____ prayed with the family regularly if he was present.

4. _____ taught me how to use tools and would help me with my projects.

5. _____ never overly punished (bruises or worse) me for doing wrong.

6. _____ would explain on a regular basis how to apply Scripture to my life.

7. _____ said on a regular basis, "I love you" or "I am proud of you."

8. _____ explained why he had to discipline me if I did something wrong.

9. _____ spent time alone reading Scripture for his own spiritual growth

10. _____ was one person I would share my deepest, most personal thoughts with.

11. _____ never caused me to worry about which "dad" would show up when he came home (an out-of- control dad, a kind and gentle dad, an erratic dad, an impatient and irritable dad, etc.).

12. _____ often would assist the church or community by doing projects designed to help those in need.

13. _____ always "had my back" if I was wrongfully accused of doing something I did not do.

14. _____ rarely yelled or screamed at me when upset.

15. _____ led by example.

16. _____ often asked me for my opinion on things I was familiar with.

17. _____ did not act like a dictator in our home (things did not have to be "his way or the highway").

18. _____ was the same person in public as he was at home.

19. _____ attended, if possible, most of my extracurricular activities.

20. _____ was always faithful to Mom.

21. _____ prayed the blessing at our meals or took the lead in having a family member do so.

22. _____ made sure I knew he was glad I was his son.

23. _____ never gave me reason to be fearful of him.

24. _____ regularly read to me bedtime Bible stories when I was a young boy.

25. _____ treated everyone in the home with respect.

26. _____never evoked unusually harsh punishment on me.

27. _____ was faithful in attending church.

28. _____ always made me feel wanted.

29. _____ never "lashed out" at me when upset.

30. _____ explained to me how to become a Christian.

Scoring:

Transfer the number you put beside each statement to the chart below

Father-Son Relationship:	Father's Physicality	Father's Spiritual Input
1. _____	2. _____	3. _____
4. _____	5. _____	6. _____
7. _____	8. _____	9. _____
10. _____	11. _____	12. _____
13. _____	14. _____	15. _____
16. _____	17. _____	18. _____
19. _____	20. _____	21. _____
22. _____	23. _____	24. _____
25. _____	26. _____	27. _____
28. _____	29. _____	30. _____

Total: _____   _____   _____

Percentage: _____   _____   _____

Note: To find the percentage divide 40 into the total from each column.

Sample: If any one category were to total 22, divide by 40 (total number if every question were answered with a "4") and you get 55 percent.

Interpretation:

If your percentage score falls between 85 and 100 percent, odds are you may have, on occasion, witnessed some disappointments with your dad in this area, however no lingering wounds exist. In this category you gave your dad an A.

If your percentage score falls between 64 and 84 percent, you may have witnessed some negative patterns in your dad's behavior; however you are aware of his "humanness" and you have made your own choices on how you will lead in this area. In this category, you gave your dad a B.

If your percentage score falls between 37 and 63 percent, you most likely experienced a Father Wound in this area that may impede your daily life and will definitely affect your relationships, especially with family. In this category, you gave your dad a C.

If your percentage score falls between 16 and 36 percent, your Father Wound in this area is very pronounced and has caused you to consciously, or unconsciously, exhibit resentment or apathy toward your dad. In this category, you gave your dad a D.

If your percentage score falls between 0 and 15 percent, your wound in this area is so severe that you have repressed your feelings toward your dad in this area, or you may have transferred your anger to other entities. In this category, you gave your dad an F.

MOVING FORWARD

Socrates gave a bedrock of beneficial advice when he simply said, "Know thyself." That is where things have to start. Because if you don't know—or you're not willing to admit—where you are, you'll never get to where you need to be.

If you were fortunate enough to have come out of the assessment with very little, if any, indication of Father Wounds, you are most blessed. If your father is still living, now would be a great time to pick up the phone and call him to tell him you love him and how thankful you are for the job he did in fathering. If you can think of a couple of specific things you could tell him for which you are thankful in how he led you, mentored you, guided you, or loved and cared for you, be sure to tell him. It will make his day—and for that matter, probably his month and year as well! Try to make expressing your appreciation to him a regular event at least a couple of times a year. That way, you'll never find yourself in a position of saying something like, "If only I had taken the opportunity to tell Dad how much he meant to me and how much I loved him—but, now it's too late."

As to the book, be sure to read on so that you'll be equipped to help others repair the results of Father Wounds, and you'll be cautioned of things to avoid in your own life so that you don't cause Father Wounds—either intentionally or unintentionally.

If, on the other hand, you found that the assessment indicates that you most likely have experienced Father Wounds, read on because this book was written especially for you! The desire is to give you helpful steps in understanding why they happen, as well as how to be healed and restored from them. It may be a tough journey, but it will be a trip you'll be glad you took and you'll welcome the results it can bring.

I applaud you for having the courage to face the issue and ask the tough questions.

Finally, be sure that you remember this assessment is simply an indicator and *not* an infallible tool. It is meant simply to give you an indication of something that may need more assessment and attention. For that, Rick and I highly suggest you see a solid, mature ministry leader or credentialed Christian therapist. (We highly recommend a Christian therapist because we strongly believe that the worldview they bring to the table is critical when it comes to counsel and help. Rick and I are both unapologetically and unwaveringly Christian when it comes to worldview.)

NOTES

4 Why so Many Wounded, and Why so Many Wounds

With so many saying they have experienced Father Wounds in their growing-up journey, the question begs to be asked: *Why?* What were some of the root causes that affected so many dads, stepdads, and father figures contributing to their causing Father Wounds in the lives of their kids? That is a huge question with more answers than we can possibly address in the brief space here, but let's consider at least a few of the major contributors in the last century or so.

. . . .

WHO SAYS YOU CAN'T TAKE THE BOY OUT OF THE COUNTRY?

While America, in its early decades, developed cities that would increasingly become population centers, it was the farm—rural America—that would primarily shape its people. Fathers would work side by side with their family members on a daily basis. Life was shared at every level—hard work, laughter, cooperative efforts, and interdependency. Dads were actively engaged with their kids, and they saw him in all types of situations—how he responded to difficult situations, his work ethic, his patience (or lack of it), his thankfulness (or its absence), and so on. You get the picture.

Time with dad began at young ages as every family member was needed to get both the chores and the work done. "What's the difference between those two categories?" you ask. *Chores* were all those things that had to get done within the home for the family to be able to function effectively. Things needed to be in their place, and there was a place for everything. Cleaning up was a must to avoid a mess. Washing clothes and bedding was essential to hygiene. Food had to be prepared; dishes, pots and pans washed; floors swept. That was *inside* the house!

And then the *work* began. That was *outside* the house in the field. And dad took a front and center role there. There is something key about "presence" while involved in meaningful tasks that binds people's lives together.

In 1800, 94 percent of Americans lived in the rural areas of the nation. By 1900 it was still a majority, at approximately 60 percent. But a massive transition was taking place. More and more dads were moving from the farm to the shop, and while the rural areas continued to grow, the urban areas were growing much more rapidly. Manufacturing, which had occurred primarily on the farm, increasingly shifted to mass production and factories. Electricity began to revolutionize living, as well as working, and came to the urban areas first. Add the invention of the car—which would bring better roads and transportation comfort primarily in the cities and increasingly replace the horse—and more and more fathers moved away from the farm and home for their work patterns.

As the 1900s exploded onto the scene, the movement of urban neighborhoods began to surge across the city landscapes as more and more moved from the farm to the city for mass employment, the convenience of improved transportation, and the wave of nearby shopping. As with every change decision, there were gains—and losses. Dad was increasingly lost from a consistent presence in the field and home, and the groundwork for the increasingly absent father (physically, emotionally, interactively) was laid, often without the growing population understanding what was happening relationally.

By the 2010 census 80.7 percent of Americans had moved to urban areas,[6] and thus the required interaction of the family found in rural living had also migrated away in many homes.

AND THE WARS RAGED ON

With the dawn of the twentieth century came the continuing results of the industrial revolution—the societal shifts of urbanization and international tensions that increased worldwide and led to multiple devastating conflicts, including World War I, World War II, the Korean Conflict, Vietnam, and the wars of the Middle East.

Tragically, especially in the twentieth century, war became an increasing part of global life in an increasingly complex world. And with war came the devastating carnage of men's lives, especially. Many dads were pulled from their families by both volunteering and, throughout some years, the draft. Many single young men would be swept up into the global struggles and either wounded or affected by what we know today as

---

6   *Reuters News*, March 26, 2012, "More Americans Move to Cities in Past Decade Census."

post-traumatic stress disorder. This trauma they would carry into their future marriages and families. Many others who entered wars as married men either had not had children yet or had children who were born while they were at war. Many would return carrying with them physical and emotional trauma from the conflicts and would be faced with another trauma: having to adjust to fatherhood and resuming marriage while carrying a lot of baggage.

The horror of battle seared men's memory banks with images they could not shake regardless of how hard they tried—images that would keep them awake due to nightmare-saturated fitful sleep. Friends and fellow soldiers had been beside them at one moment and blown apart the next. Observing crippling wounds became a way of life. Enemy against enemy far too often became hand-to-hand combat from which only one would walk away. Following such horrific trauma, men would find themselves attempting to "fit back in" to civilization and normalcy upon their return home, often to no avail.

To get a sense of what many men carried into their marriages and families, just recall scenes from or watch the following movies afresh:

WORLD WAR II	KOREAN WAR	VIETNAM WAR
• *Hacksaw Ridge*	• *Pork Chop Hill*	• *We Were Soldiers*
• *Saving Private Ryan*	• *The Front Line*	• *Apocalypse Now*
• *Patton*	• *The Steel Helmet*	• *The Killing Fields*
• *Pearl Harbor*	• *War Is Hell*	• *Full Metal Jacket*
	• *Into the Fire*	

And then think of the statistics of each conflict and the resultant deaths and wounded soldiers so many men watched, and were unable to forget:

27

WORLD WAR I	116,708 U.S. military killed	204,000 Wounded
WORLD WAR II	407,300 U.S. military killed	671,846 Wounded
KOREAN WAR	33,600 U.S. military killed	92,134 Wounded
VIETNAM WAR	58,209 U.S. military killed	153,303 Wounded
AFGHANISTAN	20,000+ U.S. military killed	22,000+ Wounded
IRAQ	4,500 U.S. military killed	32,000+ Wounded

The *Greatest Generation* would often return, suppressing their memories to the best of their ability. Their response of choice would be silence, not engaging in discussions about the trauma, just "keeping it inside."

The Vietnam vets returned to a nation that was often critical, demeaning, and ungrateful for their service. Having given their all, they often felt they returned to a nation that offered nothing but disdain in return. Many who should have expressed gratitude expressed only hate and criticism

In the years that followed, world conflicts in which America was involved continued to proliferate. And with the conflicts came injuries that would change life forever. With medical science that improved exponentially, many wounds that would have been mortal in earlier years proved to be survivable—especially in Afghanistan and Iraq. Yet those who survived them returned with gargantuan hurdles to climb as they strove to adjust back into a productive life.

And with so many emotional and physical wounds from increased warfare came greatly increased Father Wounds.

. . . .

WHEN THE BOTTOM DROPPED OUT

Black Tuesday—March 29, 1929.

The bottom dropped out of the economic well-being of homes, families, individuals, and the nation as a whole.

The nation had been giddy about its future. The Roaring Twenties had been filled with an attitude of living life "full out," with manifold new inventions and technical innovations and a sense of invincibility. Debt skyrocketed as people embraced a "buy now, pay later" philosophical lifestyle.

Within months twelve million were unemployed, with twelve thousand daily losing their jobs at the height of the Great Depression. National employment would hit a staggering 25 percent.

Since banks had no such thing as federally insured deposits, many lost everything as banks faltered and then collapsed. Over 10 percent of the nation's banks would fold.

As a result of these two staggering realities, many men would become hobos traveling the rails of America in search of work, food, and dignity. Many others would lose their homes and be reduced to living in shanty towns on public land with their fellow destitute citizens. Fifty percent of children would not have adequate nutrition, shelter, or medical care.

In the Dakotas, Nebraska, Kansas, Oklahoma, and New Mexico, farms and family ranches would become a dust bowl due to severe drought. John Steinbeck's *Grapes of Wrath* and *Of Mice and Men* would describe the devastation on people's lives as over one hundred million acres were destroyed, preventing fruitful crop production, and another three million people would become impoverished. Foreclosures and bankruptcies ripped away acreage that had been in families for decades.

The top marginal tax rate soared from 25 percent to 63 percent.

When a man's greatest need is being *adequate*, and his greatest fear is being *inadequate*, imagine how many men experienced wounds in their self-respect, self-image, and confidence. As a result, many pulled within themselves, becoming stoic and distant. Legions lashed out in anger and fury regarding circumstances they could not control. Still others abandoned families, while many others decided to end it all by suicide.

And those wounds would often be passed on to children—many of whom would become future fathers.

THE MODERN WORKPLACE AND STRAINED MARRIAGES

As the twentieth century progressed, new pressures arose within the American family. Dads traveled farther and farther to work, and yet upon returning home, they still had the normal responsibilities of head of the home waiting. Less and less time was available to spend with the kids, and the normal prolonged interaction that came with the days of rural life vanished.

More and more wives and mothers entered the workplace as families attempted to "keep up with the Joneses" and expand their ability to meet the rising costs of urban life. This often added strain to households, not simply because some felt women shouldn't work, but because husbands and wives would fight against ruthless schedules and demands to keep their relationships as husbands and wives, moms and dads strong and healthy. Dads would find themselves facing increasing expectations with less and less time to meet them.

As a result, the haunting words of Harry Chapin's song "Cat's in the Cradle" became increasingly characteristic of too many homes. You may well remember this sobering ballad. If you haven't listened to it lately, or if somehow you have missed it in the journey, take a moment and hit the internet. Read the lyrics or listen to the song. You'll find a busy, busy dad who is trying to make a success in life. He always has time for business and work but, tragically, very little for his son. Yet his little boy continually aspires to be just like his dad when he grows up, and his smile never dims . . . until his teen years. The relationship drifts. Years later the dad tries to reconnect with the son, who has moved away and, undoubtedly, taken the baggage of Father Wounds with him.

Here are the chilling closing words of the song:

> *I've long since retired, my son's moved away I called him up just the other day . . .*
>
> *And as I hung up the phone it occurred to me . . . My boy was* ***just like me***[7]

In 1969 marriage would receive a devastating blow as California became the first state to embrace no-fault divorce. Wikipedia defines it as the following:

> ***No-fault divorce*** *is a divorce in which the dissolution of a marriage does not require a showing of wrongdoing by either party. Laws providing for no-fault divorce allow a family court to grant a divorce in response to a petition by either party of the marriage without requiring the petitioner to provide evidence that the defendant has committed a breach of the marital contract.*[8]

As marriages increasingly imploded across the nation, kids experienced increasing wounds from parents' choices. Marriage too often became another "disposable" commodity. And kids were often left wondering what they had done to cause their parents' divorce!

---

7   Harry Chapin, *Cat's in the Cradle,* Cat's in the Cradle lyrics © Warner Chappell Music, Inc.

8   Wikipedia, s.v. "No-fault divorce," last edited December 2, 2019, 04:05, https://en.wikipedia.org/wiki/No-fault_divorce.

THE GREAT SOCIETY DIDN'T TURN
OUT TO BE SO GREAT AFTER ALL

New into his presidency, following the world-shaking assassination of John Kennedy in Dallas, Lyndon B. Johnson would shake the nation again on the campus of the University of Michigan. On that day in 1964 he would launch, arguably, the most intrusive government expansion in the history of the United States. From it government would explode with new departments such as Transportation and Housing and Urban Development. On the "good intention" side, such helps as food stamps would become a staple to aid many poor people. But on the tragic side, many would cease to work and, like with any entitlement, abuse and fraud would skyrocket.

Yet promises would roll down like rivers, projecting a utopian future—racial discrimination would become a thing of the past, poverty would be eradicated, public schools would become the envy of the world, families would experience unprecedented stability, and Uncle Sam would become the answer to all problems and the provider of all needs.

As a result, many in urban and inner-city settings would be negatively affected far beyond anything that could have been imagined.

Below are just some of the developments that turned out to be far less than "Great":

- Two massive entitlement programs, Medicare and Medicaid, would begin to explode in growth and, with time, would face financial instability.
- The government would increasingly "borrow" the reserves for these programs, continually pushing down the road a day of reckoning.

- Medicaid recipients grew from four million in 1966 to over seventy million in 2018, while Medicare increased from twenty million in 1966 to over sixty million over the same period.
- Governmental funding actually incentivized single mothers not to marry the fathers of their children so that they might receive greater financial support.
- Fatherlessness in the inner city—and especially in black communities—exponentially exploded, reaching 72 percent of all black children.
- Forty percent of all children were born to unmarried mothers (in 1963 more than 90 percent of babies were born to married parents).
- Cohabitation skyrocketed.
- Marriage collapsed, especially among low-income communities.
- The poverty rate didn't significantly improve; in fact it is now higher for those under the age of 18 than in 1966—even after $22 trillion being spent over 50 years.

Imagine the number of wounds resulting from these broken promises, de-motivators, entitlements that created dependency rather than independency, and resulted in millions of broken marriages, homes, neighborhoods, and communities. And those breakdowns would be passed on to kids of the following generations.

A PERSONAL PERSPECTIVE

As I look back in my life, I see parents who were kids in the Great Depression and witnessed the stresses up close and personal. My adopted dad wasn't even privileged to be in a family during this period with a married mom and dad. Rather, he was raised by a grandmother and alcoholic grandfather. I remember him talking about how he often wondered from where the next meal would come, if he was loved, and if there was any hope that life could get better.

He served in the Navy during World War II, but he would never talk about it. On rare occasions he would mention he saw some terrible stuff, but he never expressed what the "stuff" was. Instead, he just "stuffed it."

Being raised poor in a small, rough river town, he experienced the breakdown of the family firsthand.

As an adult, his work as a heavy equipment operator on construction jobs would take him away from home a lot. Making matters more difficult, when he was home, he really wasn't home—he was often too tired to be engaged.

But worst of all, he had wounds from his own growing up that naturally traveled along with him as he established his own marriage and family. Father Wounds have a way of doing that.

As I grew up I watched him regularly express signs of searching and seeking for his own healing and significance—even when I didn't understand at the time that is what was happening. His feelings of inadequacy and inferiority, engrained through difficult adolescent and teen years, surfaced repeatedly. And as a result, he struggled with intimacy in relationships, even within the family structure.

What I witnessed and experienced growing up, I would inevitably find influencing my journey as well as I moved toward, and into, adulthood. I did not understand at the time that Father Wounds tend to be multigenerational until someone puts a *stop* to the repeating cycle. Facing those Father Wounds left me with a big decision: What would I do about healing from—and preventing—Father Wounds in my own journey?

No one could make that decision but me!

NOTES

5 Fathers in Search of Solidity and Significance

I LOVE THE WILD outdoors. Regardless of what part of the world it may be, get me out into the arenas where hunting and fishing take place, and there is something almost magical that happens within me. It's where life makes sense and conflicting issues come together in my mind; where I find answers to struggles, questions, and challenges; and where I learn a lot about myself.

There is nothing like the feeling of navigating the ridges of the Rockies at 9,000 to 10,000 feet in search of one of the most majestic animals known to man—the bull elk. Quietly creeping through the darkened tree line, smelling the scent of evergreen trees and sage, making an occasional cow call, and straining to listen for the regal sound of an answering bugling bull can make a man feel alive in the innermost "wildness" of his soul. Pushing himself on the steep inclines, guarding his steps against missteps, and keeping his eyes peeled for any slight movement that could be one of nature's most royal mammals make every one of the senses come alive and function at full force. A man finds himself feeling that he is finally traversing a geography that more closely resembles the topography of his soul!

Equally, I've found my soul stretched and challenged by hours spent on the Serengeti trailing the king of the jungle. The arid bush and scrub trees of seemingly never-ending sandy soil and brush. Eyes constantly searching the unending vegetation and foliage for movement, for predator eyes staring back. Ears straining to hear a roar that can carry for five miles. It all keeps one's senses on full alert. These cats can run at fifty miles per hour and leap up to thirty-six feet, so full and total attention is required to avoid the hunter becoming the hunted. There is a thrill beyond words when you find yourself hunting for an animal that can equally hunt you, and every synapse is firing at full force as a man feels more alive than he ever imagined possible while merely walking the concrete jungles of the metropolitan areas back home. There is a part of every man that yearns for life that requires his best—not merely his least, or even average.

Yet again, sit in a deer blind quietly awaiting daybreak. Make your way into your position, being extremely careful not to make a sound or leave your scent hanging on vegetation you may carelessly brush against. Silently position yourself in the enveloping darkness while nature prepares for the sun's reappearance as it begins to spread its fingers over the eastern horizon. As you watch and listen to the world awaken with the morning light and nature sounds, your eyes strain through the receding darkness searching for the movement of deer before they retreat into the darkened woods and heavy thicket as the day dawns around you. And, the whole while, there is something deep within you yearning for parts of your inner being to awaken as well. I know—I've been there.

I have done all of these and in the process have made an important discovery about myself. In each of these cases, and more, I have found that the thing being sought was not simply the thrill of the hunt but, equally, the search for wholeness and significance in my own soul—and a sense of *being adequate* as a man. The ultimate prize was not simply a trophy for my man cave or meat for the freezer but a discovery of myself as a man, a husband, and a father. I would repeatedly find that mere *success* was not satisfying or fulfilling in any lasting manner. Similarly, in my work, plaques on the wall, mention in media articles, or bigger offices and increased responsibility wasn't found to be sufficient. I wanted, even more, to have a significant impact in my key roles as husband, father, leader, and—hopefully—a balanced man. Gradually I was learning that relationships were ultimately more important that accomplishments.

But searching for yourself is often not an easy or straightforward journey. And it's interesting to note some of the arenas men focus in as they strive for the search—sports, work, adventures. I heard the head of Delta Airlines make a statement that captured the search. He said, "Sometimes the best way to find yourself is to lose yourself in an adventure or experience."

In my journey to grow and deal with some of the giants in my life, I discovered the unsettling truth that it is possible for a man to be a recognized and visible success in the workplace while being a colossal failure at home. Dads can reach the top of the ladder vocationally, while crashing to the bottom of the ladder parentally and relationally at home. While experiences like those referred to above can reach deep down into a man's inner core, they fail to come close to the wonder of a dad delighting in his kids, regularly acknowledging his love and pride for them, and watching their hungry response to such affirmation. There indeed is no greater "trophy."

EVERY MAN IS ON A SEARCH

Recently I was speaking in the Great Falls, Montana, area and was reminded how much I love the West. There is something magical about the ruggedness of it that seems to call to the soul of most men I know. A wildness and expanse that seems to embody the term "Big Sky" and which symbolically reminds every man of the limitless possibilities that life, as it was originally created, has to offer.

Taking advantage of some free time in an early afternoon, I set out to hike along the river's edge trail as it skirted the beautiful Missouri River. The river's falls were mesmerizing to my sight as my footsteps fell along the footpath. I couldn't help but imagine Lewis and Clark as they traversed that way long before modern man had put his hand and ingenuity to the rough-hewn wilderness. Was the only thing they were searching for new, uncharted land? Or previously undiscovered passages? Or could there have been more?

Could it have been that part of what drove them to regions previously unknown and uncharted was also a search for themselves? A search to know deep down within their soul the answers to questions such as *Who am I? Why do I exist? Do I have what it takes to make a difference? Where am I going? Will I be adequate and have what it takes?*

I can't go back in time and have any way to know for sure. But knowing men the way I do, having spoken before so many, I think every man walks—and explores—with those questions partially driving their actions and directions. They are questions that every many wants answered. They haunt every man's steps. And their answers can make all the difference in a man's directions and journey.

But I do know that in my outdoor adventures across the globe, even more than I wanted to find the big game—even if I just chose to watch them, absorbed in their majestic and regal glory—I was searching for *me!* Pursuing and discovering my true self was tantamount to my searches. And the ultimate goal, strangely—and at times unacknowledged by me—was not nearly as much about getting a trophy for home as it was *about becoming a trophy of God's grace* in the hunt for life at its best.

HOW EASILY THE SEARCH
GETS THROWN OFF TRACK

But the pursuit can be easily derailed, or tripped up, for too many men. God's desire is that we come to know early—and fully—that we are His, created by His hand. And His intent is that we have a deep and growing relationship with the One who has created us. So much so, that the Scripture says that God has "set eternity in the human heart" (Ecclesiastes 3:11). The scientist Paschal said that every human has a God-shaped vacuum in his or her soul—a God-shaped hole. As a result, nothing and no one can fill that hole—only God the Creator, made known through Jesus Christ, His Son, can.

God desires that we find our identity as a son of God. And that isn't bequeathed by nationality, church membership, completed ritual, or any other man-made criteria. That comes only by relationship, and that is possible only through Jesus Christ (John 14:6). That drives home the point that I cannot discover *who* I am until I'm ready to deal with *whose* I am.

But so much baggage can prevent us from that discovery. Our true identity far too often becomes mired in two very false measurements. Several years ago, Robert McGee warned that too often

Performance + Others' Opinions = Our Identity[9]

And when a young person, especially a boy, becomes mired in attempting to establish his identity solely based on *performing* to meet his dad's (or stepdad's, or father figure's) expectations, he can

---

9   Robert S. McGee, *The Secret of Significance*, (Nashville, TN: Thomas Nelson, 2004), p. 16.

easily feel he will never live up to them or measure up. Likewise, being wounded by unhealthy opinions, criticisms, or put-downs by these authority figures can derail a young man in his search for *who he is* and *why he exists.* As a result, he will regularly feel he doesn't have what it takes to make a difference and become all that he can be. Performance, according to another's expectations—especially a dad's or stepdad's—becomes a relentless, and often ruthless, master.

One of Satan's greatest desires is for us men to miss our true identity, get enmeshed in self-doubt, and become impotent in reaching our God-given destiny. Character development is displaced by a performance trap. And as we age the performance is often job and career centered, rather than family centered. Too often men see faster "results" at work than at home. Rewards for effort seem to pay off faster in the workplace than on the home front. Appreciation is received quicker on the job than in the trenches of routine at home. So, if they are not careful, dads and stepdads can become more focused on success at work than on making a significant—and eternal—difference at home. The *major* becomes the minor. And the potentially tragic results can last for a lifetime.

I know in my own journey, I found myself often trying to prove my adequacy by covering up my inadequacy. Continually I found myself striving to earn my dad's approval and measure up to often "self-imposed" expectations. And because my dad was the "strong silent type," I was never quite sure where I stood. Whether on the sports fields or floors, academics, or whatever the activity, I wanted to measure up, to be adequate and to hear my dad, above all else, say so.

But I would find that, too, seemed to be an elusive pursuit and a moving target.

NOTES

6 What Every Child Needs in a Dad

HEALTHY DEVELOPMENT IN any child requires a dad, stepdad, or father figure who provides needed contributions through a handful of critically important roles. If one of those roles is missing, a key element, or elements, of the child's development can go missing.

And these roles are not each limited to a cookie-cutter set of specified years. Indeed, there are some seasons of development in which a certain role is more critical, but in truth, each of the roles plays a part in each season of maturing to some degree.

But when a role is diminished, ignored, or—at worst—absent, the unfortunate results are inevitable.

. . . .

PROVIDER/PROTECTOR

Every child needs a secure environment in which they feel safe, where *trust* is a key.

In order to grow in confidence, children need to know their environment is one in which they are assured that they have the ability to grow, develop, experiment, and question. They cannot be healthy and have to wonder if they will be cared for, encouraged, and affirmed.

And they shouldn't have to worry about their basic needs. Children don't have the emotional strength, in general, to carry the weight of worry as to whether they will be properly provided for and protected. That is the parents' role and responsibility. In order for children to be healthy they need to experience the security and freedom to be children.

Every child needs to know that there is an adult protector who will help them as they grow to be assured that nothing will be allowed to harm them or compromise them. There is a relief experienced within such security that affords for a buffer between the child and the many threats they experience at each stage of life.

When it comes to the home environment, the home should be a secure environment of love and encouragement, help and assistance, building-up and affirmation, and warmth and peace. Rip these away and a child becomes tentative, afraid, withdrawn, and resentful

As children move into adolescence and their teenage years, they need to know they can experience new opportunities yet be protected while doing so. Wise counsel, not suffocating control, must be offered to help navigate the challenging terrain of the teenage years. Teens need to be able to increasingly make decisions for themselves within the safety net of support, reasonable freedom, and clear boundaries. And they definitely need a way out when they may find themselves in circumstances they know are not wise and in which they need a route of escape, while still "saving face."

In our family, we always told our adolescent or teen kids, "If you ever find yourself at a party or gathering where you feel uncomfortable and sense you need to find a way out, feel free to say you really feel bad and are afraid you're getting sick. Call us and we'll come and get you and no one will know anything contrary."

And that offer was acted upon several times. But our kids always felt they had an "escape hatch" if needed, while still able to "save face."

As teens go through their most tumultuous years of puberty, hormones, and emotional conflicts, they need a dad who will stand both **WITH** them and **AGAINST** the many forces that assail them.

WITH them in believing in their potential. Affirming their strengths. Encouraging their growing journey toward independence, while constantly offering support as needed. Loving them for who they are, not simply for how they perform. And engaging in those things that are important to them—not simply what is convenient or comfortable for dad.

AGAINST the forces that strive to pull them away from the core base of faith and family. Helping to remind them of what in life is important and *why*, based on family values. Encouraging the opportunities to learn, grow, and experience life-changing opportunities and education, while never supporting a child taking up the position of being a "perpetual victim," living dependent on the government, or developing a perspective of always seeing the glass of life as half-empty.

Therefore, it is critical at each stage for kids to see their dad as *provider* and *protector*.

NURTURER

Every life has a basic need to be nurtured—to be continually encouraged, built up, and believed in. And there is amazing strength extended into the life of a child when the strength that comes from dad is affirming, encouraging, and liberating.

Boys so desperately long to hear their dad say "I'm proud of you" and to know it's not just for how they perform on the athletic field or floor. To have a father wrap his arms around his son's shoulders and pull him close or slap him on the back in congratulations for who he is, as well as for whatever he may have just accomplished, is an inherent desire in the heart of every boy.

Boys are born with eternal questions of *Do I have what it takes? Am I adequate to meet life's challenge?* It must be remembered that as boys mature, their greatest fear will become inadequacy. That disquieting nagging will go with them all the way into their own marriages and families. *Am I adequate as a husband? Do I have what it takes as a father? Will I be adequate physically, emotionally, sexually, financially, vocationally?* Such nagging questions will haunt them off and on, repeatedly, for the totality of life's journey.

Girls, on the other hand, will be born with a core life question, *Am I secure?* For her, security will become a core anchor in life. It is what will help her become a wife, mother, and homemaker that provides a "nest" in which the family feels *at home, relaxed, joyful.*

As a part of her anchoring core she will also want to know that dad loves her and that in his eyes, she is as pretty as a princess. Regardless of how old she may become, there will always be a little girl inside of her wanting to know, *Daddy, am I pretty? Daddy, do you love me just the way I am?* And when marriage comes, she'll have the same internal questions regarding her husband's view of her.

Dr. David Stoop says that the impact of the nurturer is especially critical between the ages of birth and age five.[10] In the view of many dads, these are years they feel aren't that critical because their children are "too young." Yet nothing could be more incorrect. These are formative foundation years for everything else that

---

10 David Stoop, *Making Peace with Your Father* (Grand Rapids, Michigan: Revell, 1992, 2004), p. 51.

46

will follow. And if missed or squandered, they are extremely hard to recapture and rebuild.

THE BOUNDARY MAKER/ENFORCER

Every life needs boundaries, but several temperaments have difficulty establishing them. And all of us need coaching on how to do it effectively, especially as we grow up.

Stop and think a moment of just how important boundaries are. What would a basketball court, football or soccer field, or baseball diamond be without them? If roller coasters had no set tracks, what would the ride be like? Can you imagine the chaos that would result in the ownership of property if clearly marked boundaries were absent?

God established this reality with His first kids in the garden. The boundaries were given not to limit their joy but to protect their freedom. They were an indicator not of God's repressive tendencies but rather of His love and protection. It was not for His comfort but for their security.

Rather than zeroing in on what Adam and Eve were to avoid (the tree of the knowledge of good and evil), take a moment to focus on how much freedom they were given. The garden in its entirety was their playground environment, and only one small area was their "out of bounds." Don't you find it ironic how we can blow out of proportion boundaries that are actually established for our good?

Had God's first created couple learned to live within the safety of the boundaries they were given, they would have established a pattern of making future boundaries of their own for their own good, as well as for their offspring. But parents cannot successfully exercise what they themselves have not personally lived by.

It is why kids often feel regarding their parents, "I can't hear what you are saying because your actions drown out your words."

Sadly, with human nature being what it is, we cannot be surprised by the first couple's focus being not on their freedoms but on what they felt were their *unfair* limitations. They questioned what God must be "withholding" from them rather than celebrating their otherwise limitless run of paradise. Their focus became questioning why God was holding back something that must be great from them. If only they would have realized that when they transgressed God's boundaries, the resultant consequences would have far-reaching ramifications—not only in their lives, but in that of their family as well.

Likewise, children must learn not only the reality of boundaries but also the consequences for not acknowledging and obeying them. These consequences are not harsh punishment but logical forewarned outcomes. Therefore, whenever boundaries are set with children, the resultant consequences should be clearly established and understood by the child. Then, when boundaries are crossed, the appropriate consequences need to be experienced, not sloughed off, delayed, or forgotten. When that happens, kids learn that boundaries at any stage in life can be ignored or violated and there will be no significant ramifications.

Just as the loving heavenly Father sat boundaries for the good of His children, so every earthly father must set them for his. This is critical if he wants them to function well and maturely as they grow. If they don't experience them at home, they will be ill-prepared to face them in the numerous arenas of life. Children will encounter boundaries in school, sports, social organizations, clubs, jobs, you name it. And what better place to learn this reality than in the safety and protection of the home training ground?

That is why twice in Deuteronomy God said to the men of Israel (and their families) to not only acknowledge the reality of boundaries but also convey them to their children as a critical preparation for a significant and successful future:

> *"Listen, O Israel! The Lord is our God, the Lord alone. And you must love the Lord your God with all your heart, all your soul, and all your strength. And you must commit yourselves wholeheartedly to these commands that I am giving you today. Repeat them again and again to your children. Talk about them when you are at home and when you are on the road, when you are going to bed and when you are getting up. Tie them to your hands and wear them on your forehead as reminders. Write them on the doorposts of your house and on your gates."* (Deuteronomy 6:4–9 NLT)
> *"Take to heart all the words of warning I have given you to-day. Pass them on as a command to your children so they will obey every word of these instructions. These instructions are not empty words—they are your life! By obeying them you will enjoy a long life in the land you will occupy."* (Deuteronomy 32:46–47 NLT)

Fathers are to be the point men here, setting the course for the following generations.

This in no way permits the simplistic answer of "Because I said so" by dads. That will never work over the long haul without engendering deep-seated anger and animosity. Boundaries require clarity of understanding as to what is meant, why they exist, and the consequences that will result if they are breached. When that occurs, children grow in understanding their responsibility of walking through life wisely, and not just "getting by."

One last caution: empty promises of what will happen if boundaries are breached, and then failing to enforce them, only create a child who grows to believe that they can ignore any and every boundary whatsoever, wherever, whenever—at no risk. As the heavenly Father set the guidelines and warned of the consequences, so for the good of the child, the earthly father is needed in the life of a child to take the lead in modeling the importance of boundaries and how to navigate them wisely. This will prove invaluable to aiding the child in navigating well their life's journey.

This role, while important at every stage of the child's journey, is especially critical during the grade school and early teen years.

COACH

In the early years parents are needed to be directive as they significantly help mold a child's actions, attitudes, and choices. But as the journey through childhood and adolescence progresses, that same parent must move from a more directive stance to an increasingly coaching stance. This is especially true of dads with sons.

What is meant by a role as coach? It is a role that is natural and ubiquitous in numerous life arenas as the child matures. None is more quickly to come to mind than sports. Whether it be baseball, soccer, gymnastics, field hockey, football, or whatever other endeavor is named, every team comes "prepackaged" with a common element: a coach.

Simply stated, a good coach is one who offers support and assistance to those he (or she) coaches in order to help their players develop and implement skills, execute meaningful change, and achieve desired goals. Ask any young man who plays any sport as he grows up who the most influential people were in his life's journey, and coaches will often be among the top mentioned. Why? Because they are very engaged, intentionally helping the child experience progress, and encouraging them in their defeats and celebrating in their successes. A key part of the *engagement* and *intentionality* is found in helping the learner develop new understanding and skills.

Dads have a great opportunity here to aid sons in navigating the tough, and often challenging, rapids of adolescence and teen years. But where is a dad to start?

An easy yet very productive beginning point is *encouragement and affirmation.* The dad who is constantly looking for things he can affirm and encourage on a daily basis reaps great dividends relationally with his son. Conversely, the dad who finds it easier to find what is wrong or weak in a son's life will reap alienation, anger, and resentment.

What a son desires deeply in his soul to hear from his dad, more than anything else, is how proud his dad is of him—not just how he performs (e.g., on the athletic field or floor), but far greater regarding the character by which he lives.

Kevin recalled, with moist eyes, how his father regularly put him down and criticized him during his high school years. "It seemed like I couldn't do enough to make him proud of me. And he never complimented me on who I was, or who I was becoming. It made me feel like I could never measure up. And so it went. Even on the athletic field I could hear my dad derogatorily yelling from the stands when I would drop a pass or get tackled before the goal line. But suddenly, it would take a 180-degree turn when I made the hard catch or when I stretched across the goal. Then suddenly my dad was screaming, 'That's my boy! Did you see that? He's a chip right off the old block of his dad!' I soon learned the only time my dad seemed to be proud of me was when it made *him* look good."

Dads who look for at least one character quality in their sons (and daughters) to affirm and/or encourage daily will see their sons becoming increasingly confident, self-assured, and happy in their lives.

In the recent Christmas season, it was driven home to me just how important this is in the life of a child.

I discovered that in colonial America many families had brought some brightly colored plates from their European homeland. A tradition began to develop that placed such a plate at the seat of a guest who was visiting or a family member on a special day. With time, the tradition reportedly began to include the sharing by everyone present of things they appreciated about the one being honored—often character qualities.

My friend Jimmy Sites introduced me to this wonderful experience while hunting overseas. Every evening as people gathered around the table, the red plate charger (a bigger plate placed under the main dinner plate) would be awaiting at the place of someone different. And at a certain point of the evening meal, Jimmy would call our attention to verbally honor the one who had the special plate (charger). The focus was never about what they had done or accomplished on the hunt but rather about who they were as a person.

So, with our son, daughter-in-law, and their three kids visiting with us for Christmas, I slipped a red charger under the dinner plate of one of our eight-year-old grandsons. The buzz as they arrived at the table was, "What's the red plate for?" "You'll find out before dinner is over," I responded. "And I think you'll like it!"

As we approached dessert, I told them the history of the special plate. Then I made clear that each night of the Christmas season the plate would be placed at a different person's place, and that night each person around the table would hear everyone else tell at least one character quality they valued and appreciated in the life of the one who sat at the special plate. As everyone, starting with his twin brother, Colt, went around the table and told Jaxson at least one quality they valued in his life, you could actually see his chest began to swell. A smile increasingly spread across his face. And, with no exaggeration, his face began to glow.

Needless to say, I broke into laughter the following evening when I walked into the dining room, helping my wife get everything set for the upcoming dinner, only to discover that Colt had preceded me and made sure the red charger was at his place for the coming meal! That said it all! And not to be outdone, our granddaughter, Georgia Grace, did the same thing the next night.

Later, my son Bryan said to me privately, "Dad, if you had told me ahead of time what you planned I would probably have cautioned you that I didn't think the kids would have responded to it or gotten its meaning. I was stunned to watch how they responded to it every night. It was great!"

There is nothing sweeter to a child's ears, regardless of the age, than to hear affirmation, encouragement, and praise!

AN IDEA FOR DADS: BECOMING A BETTER COACH

But what about developing new skills or reaching established goals? Here's an idea for dads' coaching efforts. What dad is not concerned with his kids making wise choices when it comes to choosing friends and ultimately choosing a mate? That will require knowledge of what character qualities make great friends (or a great mate) and which ones undermine success.

There is no better place to get a base than the biblical book of Proverbs, which clearly delineates among three types of people: wise, foolish, and evil. A simple study clearly outlines the differences. What if you were to read through the thirty-one-chapter biblical book for yourself in a good modern translation, discover the characteristics for yourself (What dad couldn't improve on his own discernment and people skills?), and then pick a time weekly to cover the journey step-by-step on a kid's basis with your son

(or daughter). It can be done at a restaurant, at home, in a park—
you name it. The place is only limited by your creativity. And it
doesn't have to be long, or your kids will go into a coma! Bite-sized
sessions over time far exceed trying to drink from a fire hose.

And to give you a running start, dad, here is a sampling of what
you will find (this is by no means comprehensive). I came across
these lists in a great book by Dr. Henry Cloud titled *Necessary
Endings*. It launched me on my own study, and I hope it will start
you on yours.

WISE PEOPLE (People Who Choose to Live God's Way)

- When you give them feedback, they listen, take it in, and
  adjust their behavior accordingly.
- When you give them feedback, they embrace it positively.
  There is some sort of appreciation for the feedback, as they
  see it as something of value, even if it is hard to hear.
- They own their performance, problems, and issues and
  take responsibility for them without excuses or blame.
- Your relationship is strengthened as a result of giving them
  feedback. They thank you for it and see you as someone
  who cares enough about them to have a hard conversation.
- They empathize and express concern about the results of
  their behavior on others.
- They show remorse.
- In response to feedback, they go into future-oriented problem-solving mode. "I see this. How can I do better in the
  future?"
- They do not allow problems that have been addressed to
  turn into patterns. They change. They adjust and fix them.[11]

11 Cloud, Henry. *Necessary Endings* (New York: Harper Collins, 2010),
pp. 129, 130.

FOOLISH PEOPLE (People Who Choose to Live Their Own Way, Ignoring God's)

- When given feedback, they are defensive and immediately come back at you with a reason why it is not their fault.
- When a mistake is pointed out, they externalize the mistake and blame someone else.
- Unlike the wise person, with whom talking through issues strengthens your relationship, with the foolish person, attempts to talk about problems create, conflict, alienation, or a breach in the relationship.
- They often use minimization, trying to in some way convince you that "it's not that bad" or "this really isn't the problem that you think it is. It's not that big a deal."
- They rationalize, giving reasons why their performance was certainly understandable.
- Excuses are rampant, and they never take ownership of the issue.
- Their emotional response has nothing to do with remorse; instead they get angry at you for being on their case.
- They begin their response with "Well, you . . ." and get you off topic by pointing out your flaws.
- They have little or no awareness or concern for the pain or frustration that they are causing others or the mission.
- Their emotional stance toward getting corrected is opposite to that of the wise person. Their stance is one of anger, disdain, or some other fight-or-flight response.
- They see themselves as the victim, and they see the people who confront them as persecutors for pointing out the problem. They feel like the morally superior victim and often find someone to rescue them and agree with how bad you are for being "against" them.

- Their world is divided into the good guys and the bad guys. The good ones are the ones who agree with them and see them as good, and the bad ones are the ones who don't think they are perfect.[12]

EVIL PEOPLE (People Who Live Without Regard to God's Ways and Guidelines—and Whom Are Even Often Antagonistic to Them)

- They are not reasonable.
- Their desire is to hurt others and do destructive things. So, you have to protect yourself.
- They like to bring others down.
- They are intentionally divisive.
- They enjoy it when someone fails and try to create the downfall of others.[13]

Try it, dad, by reading just one chapter of Proverbs a day. Start making your list of the character qualities of wise people, foolish people, and evil people. It will amaze you how your discernment sharpens and how you increasingly desire to cultivate the characteristics of the wise person. And the more you learn personally, the more well positioned and prepared you will be to help your child prepare well for life.

And Dad, you'll be amazed at how much your preparation will help you in your work!

Try it, dad, by reading just one chapter of Proverbs a day. Start making your list of the character qualities of wise people, foolish people, and evil people. It will amaze you how your discernment sharpens and how you increasingly desire to cultivate the

---

12 Ibid., pp. 134-136.
13 Ibid., pp. 142-144.

characteristics of the wise person. And the more you learn personally, the more well positioned and prepared you will be to help your child prepare well for life.

And Dad, you'll be amazed at how much your preparation will help you in your work!

NOTES

7 A Word from The Front-Row Seats

I CAN'T COUNT HOW many times I have read something by an author about real life issues and wondered if he or she knew firsthand what they were writing about. Had they ever walked in those shoes? Or, were they merely writing about something they had studied or observed?

There's just something about the authenticity of "been there, experienced that."

So allow me to share a bit of my journey.

I was born into a family as the third of three boys. We were stairsteps, one right after the other, making all three of us under the age of four.

My parents were extremely young, and my father was in the military. He was a heavy drinker and not at all thrilled about having so many kids, so young. Mom, on the other hand, was a delight, and everyone liked her due to her authentic realism and her sweet disposition.

While my mom was carrying me in the womb, her health began to decline. Let's admit it: having three children so fast and close together is a challenge for any woman! As her health grew to be a continuing struggle, she was even quietly encouraged to consider not taking me to term. But believing that God alone had the right to give or take life, carry me to term she did. And that cost her greatly, as she would die when I reached eleven months of age.

That left a young father, and former husband, with a handful that he was not sure he had bargained for, nor that he deeply desired. Besides, how would he work in his drinking and partying with three young dependents?

The ultimate conclusion came to be that when he decided to go "party hardy" he would look for someone to take us off his hands, thus giving him the freedom he so desperately desired. And when that occurred, he would go live his life, until he finished his plans or became guilty and would come back and take us into his keeping once again. And so it went, repeatedly, that we would be thrown from house to house and hand to hand. And when there wasn't anyone to take us into their care, there was always a large closet or a cellar.

And so the difficult challenges of life would continue across state lines as we moved from the East Coast back to the Midwest where his and my mother's roots had originally been. But, by that time he had reached the limit of what he could do so he decided to put us up for adoption. That would ultimately lead to my two older brothers being adopted by a family and me being left in the care of my dad.

That care wasn't very consistent. With his less-than-ideal lifestyle, life became tougher and tougher. At one point he would offer me to a lady with whom he desired to build a relationship, promising her that with me she could receive some aid for dependent children, thus giving her money she could use to open the bar she wanted to establish. Thankfully, that never came to reality.

Meanwhile, a couple in the Midwest had attempted to have

four children and lost each of them, three to miscarriages and the last to a tragic stillbirth. The stillbirth had been so traumatic—both physically and emotionally—that doctors had told the wife that she must never become pregnant again as she would likely not survive the pregnancy. This left a void of shattered dreams of family, a feeling of total inadequacy and looming depression in the young wife's heart.

Additionally, this couple was a most unlikely pair for building any type of successful marriage. The husband had been an illegitimate child born out of a tryst of a 45-year-old businessman with a 15-year-old girl. When he was born the businessman denied responsibility and paternity, and the young woman had no idea what to do with the child. Thus, she handed the boy to her mother and her mother's alcoholic husband. That would begin a long litany of heartbreaking experiences as the boy grew up in a home where he was often berated, ignored, and unjustly punished by the alcoholic grandfather.

Without a sense of family, the boy began to search for something that would fill the void. He finally came into contact with what we would today call a gang and found instant acceptance. And so a downward spiral began. Fights and skirmishes occurred often and regularly escalated into dangerous and threatening conditions. So it should have been no shock that one such incident culminated in his being stabbed in a fight as an older teen and seriously wounded. Stable and affirming relationships were simply nonexistent in his young life, with the emotional wounds even deeper than the now physical stab wound.

The wife, on the other hand, had been raised in a strict legalistic Christian household. Faith and success in Christian living was determined by what one did and didn't do. Life was lived on a performance basis. Religious rules became the measuring stick for success—or failure.

The two had met as young adults and unexpectedly experienced a mutual attraction that led to falling in love. As a most unlikely couple, they eloped and got married. Think of it: a husband from the raw side of life and a wife from the puritanical, legalistic faith tradition. It sounds like a marriage made in heaven, doesn't it?

Now, having lost four children of their own, they heard of three boys who had been thrown from house to house and place to place. When they arrived at the tough part of town where the boys were being kept and knocked on the door, they discovered that the older two had already been taken and adopted by a family and only the younger one was left. The crusty woman answering the door simply said, "The brat's in the back. If you want him, you can find him," and she walked away.

Making their way through the cluttered home they would finally find me in the backyard playing with the dirt, because that's all there was to play with. I was filthy, hadn't been bathed in a number of days, and was able to be smelled before I was seen.

In addition, the majority of my body was covered with severe impetigo. This bacterial skin infection, which in its advanced stages can be a repulsive thing to see, made me a ghastly physical site. Lack of proper hygiene and care and a total absence of cleanliness greatly exacerbated the dilemma and made me appear anything but warm and cuddly.

Despite the outward appearance and the convoluted background of the couple, I was taken into their home and we became a new family.

It sounds great, doesn't it? That means the story is "happily ever after," right?

Hardly!

Just think of the baggage that both men brought into the journey—my biological dad, as well as my adopted dad. That doesn't mean that they were bad men but merely that one had made some very poor life choices while the other had grown up through very difficult and life-altering circumstances, many beyond his control. And both brought the baggage to bear on their son—namely, me.

So, Father Wounds resulted from both sources, many of which I would not recognize for years to come.

Allow me to give you an example. Due to his tough upbringing, my adopted dad struggled to effectively and consistently show love and give affirmation. Having rarely received it, he struggled with how to give it. But being a man of character, despite his challenging history, he was committed to provide for me and my adopted mom. And so he developed a perspective that by working hard, regardless of the hours it took, and even having to be away for extended periods due to the job's demands, he proved his love by his provision.

All the years growing up I saw my adopted dad work as hard as any man I have ever known. Every morning he was up at 4:00, grabbed a quick breakfast, and then headed off to a cold or hot day of work in the construction trade. I marveled at how he could run any piece of construction equipment you could show him. He could handle any machine with surgical precision. His upper arms were as big as my thighs, and his skin was rugged and weathered.

Most often, he would not be home until significantly after dark, as the job site was often many miles away. When he did arrive, I remember with clarity how he would go take a shower, wearily eat dinner, and then go lay on the couch and watch TV—until he finally made his way to bed, only to face the same the following day.

There's no question that provision is a sign of love, but it cannot be the sole, or even primary, means of expression of that love. But my dad knew no differently. He was carrying Father Wounds of his own.

Added to all of that he was, by nature, an introvert and therefore not prone to effusively project feelings and emotions. Being quick to express love, affirmation, or encouragement was not his strength. He may well have felt them, even desired to convey them, but he struggled to express them. I firmly believe that he desired that it would "just be known" that he felt all of those things.

It is important for any of us to realize that wherever a void develops in life, something always moves to fill it. And in relationships such as these the "fillers" often become insecurity, doubt, emptiness, a drive to be accepted regardless of the cost, and even questioning of the sincerity of any and every relationship. Just as possible are the opposite reactions such as a strong will, anger, the tendency toward bullying, or an unteachable spirit.

So, as you can probably see, I experienced firsthand the reality of Father Wounds and the impact they leave on life. I also would face the decision if I would be the place at which they would stop—or if I would simply pass them on to the next generation.

AND LIFE GOES ON

As I grew up through the years, my adopted mom became "New Testament Grace" in my journey, while I saw my adopted dad more as "Old Testament Law." He was a good man but definitely a "by the rules" guy. My mom unwittingly helped enforce that view with statements like "Wait until your dad gets home; he'll set things straight" or "What do you think your father will say about that?" or "Your father won't stand for that." And thus dad got cast into the "bad" guy role and "the heavy" without anyone stopping to realize what was happening.

I've already acknowledged dad was a strong provider. He was constantly working and gone, and when he did get home, he was so exhausted he was too tired to play ball and didn't have the energy to focus on homework or the enthusiasm to hear about my latest adventure. Remember, to him, *providing was loving.*

And to many, that may make perfect sense. But when a boy needs to hear his dad say regularly and consistently, "I'm proud of you, son! You did that great! You're becoming quite the young man! I love you, and am so proud of you, for who you're growing up to be!" simply providing doesn't cut it on the emotional needs level.

No place did that become more impactful that when I became old enough to play sports and was fortunate to play in numerous competitive games. I learned a lot, matured from one level to the next, and relished the competitive drive to win.

But one thing was consistent: dad was never there. He was always away working. Providing. But what I deeply desired more than anything was his presence.

The ultimate culmination of that yearning surfaced in my teen years when playing basketball in a tough citywide league. The end of the season conference game had arrived. While I was never a great athlete, I had my occasional moments. On that particular night I had the game of my life—definitely played over my head. Everything I threw up seemed to drop in.

And we *won!*

Every one of my teammates had their dad swarming around them, slapping them on the back, hugging them in victory, and lifting them up in triumph. But my dad wasn't there. He was probably just getting home from work.

Talk about feeling like a fifth wheel! Out of step. Odd man out.

And through the years the feelings of emptiness, disappointment, and betrayal would go with me, not just from the one experience, but many others as well. And every time I saw a team triumph on TV or sat in a gym and watched it firsthand, the feelings came flooding back.

Some of you may be thinking, "But it wasn't intentional. Your dad didn't let you down on purpose. He was working to provide." And all of that is true. But in the eyes and heart of a young person, the unintentional can be as hurtful as the intentional.

And so, without intending to, I marched smartly into adulthood having wounds I did not realize I was carrying. And the inevitable result is that, to some degree, wounded people wound people. We may not mean to. It may well be unintentional. They could be small wounds, not big ones. But the terrible truth is that small wounds add up to *big* wounds with time and repetition.

Dr. Sandra Wilson graciously warns us who have experienced wounds in our childhood or adolescence:

> *When we seek to numb the pain or unseen wounds—either knowingly or unknowingly—with denial or other "emotional anesthetics," we inevitably create additional pain for ourselves and for others. Rather than acknowledging the existence of our invisible inner injuries and treating them, we often attempt to distance ourselves from them by deflecting our pain onto those around us. And, typically, we hurt others most deeply in the areas of our deepest wounding.*[14]

WHEN IT ALL CAME TO A HEAD

It's amazing how stuff that is often buried in our lives surfaces at the most unlikely and inconvenient times. As I moved into adulthood, had a family, and progressed through different jobs and leadership levels, I mistakenly thought I had dealt with baggage in my life pretty well. Honestly, I had never even heard

[14] Dr. Sandra D. Wilson, *Hurt People Hurt People* (Grand Rapids, Michigan: Discovery House, 2001), p. 31.

the term *Father Wounds*, so I simply kept plowing forward and upward.

At the age of forty-three I was shocked to be asked to lead a major task force for our denomination that was assigned to implement major changes that had been decided were needed to position it well for the twenty-first century. The task was massive. And the amazing part is that though it could have easily been a full-time assignment, like most denominations, it was to be done in spare time. So, I was charged with leading an amazingly talented group of men and women on a two-year journey of massive change, while at the same time pastoring a very large church full-time and striving to "fit" my family in as well.

Like I have heard some marines say about boot camp, "I'm glad I did it, but I don't want to ever do it again!"

To my amazement, at the end of the journey I was asked to step into the presidency of a very large mission agency that spanned North America and help chart a course for the new century. Its assignments stretched across such diverse areas as working with states to field over five thousand mission personnel, a major disaster relief force, mission education, church planting, and a TV and radio network. It was both an honor and at the same time a massively humbling step for a guy coming from such a dysfunctional background.

Having moved to Atlanta to assume the new role, I took my wife, Cheryl, to dinner one night. Being the middle of the week, there were only a few others in the establishment, so we settled in for a quiet dinner in our new city. While talking about the new responsibilities, the new home, the adjustment of our last child at home, and the overwhelming challenge ahead, I suddenly started to get emotional. Soon tears were welling in my eyes.

Cheryl asked if I was okay. Being a tough, in control guy, I simply answered, "Sure." But as we continued to talk, suddenly tears were running down my cheeks. I didn't know what was happening. Cheryl asked again if something was wrong, and I assured her there was not. But the tears continued to fall. In a short while, Cheryl said, "I'm going to pay the bill and we're going to slip out and head home. I think you need some space, and it probably needs to have some privacy."

To this day, I can't explain why what happened, happened—and especially then. But I have continually found that when things buried inside for a long time bubble to the surface, it often isn't the most convenient or comfortable time and place. Dad had died earlier that year. We had been on really good terms, but it had been a hard journey of increasing dementia. We had gone through a major relocation, a new and demanding job, the exhaustion of the two years of a full-time pastorate and leading a major national task force, the lengthy and emotionally draining interview process for the new job, and more. And suddenly, the Father Wounds from over the years had decided to raise their ugly heads at the most unpredictable of times.

So the question became, Now what?

NOTES

8 Every Rupture Needs to Be Restored

RUPTURES ARE EXPLOSIVE changes. Something that has been intact, stable, and operating as intended suddenly isn't.

I know this firsthand.

Like the time I was in a hurry, running behind schedule and committed to catching up. I thought I knew the right angle to pull out of the driveway in a hurry. After all, I'd done it many times before. And this time wouldn't be any different. The stone wall surrounding the flower bed and mailbox at the end of the driveway, where it meets the street, wouldn't be a problem—or so I thought.

The minute the front right tire hit the corner stone well of the bed I knew *this was trouble*! The exploding tire confirmed that assessment. I didn't make it twenty yards before the tilting front angle of the truck told me I'd just experienced a major rupture. And looking at the formerly beautiful stone wall, now laying in the street in shattered pieces, told me I wasn't going to make my appointment on time. Not anywhere close! Not to mention how thrilled my wife would be!

Or, just recently when I went downstairs to my office in the morning and stopped at the bottom of the stairs, staring at an adjacent wall down the hall. Something wasn't quite right. But what was it? It was the water feature on the wall. Was it new? Had Cheryl gotten a new decorative wall-mounted waterscape?

Suddenly it sunk in that the water flowing down the wall wasn't a new decorative waterscape at all. It was a leak! Something had ruptured. And I sprinted down the hall to the disaster.

A fully torn-out wall later, and with the house's entire water supply shut off, a handyman friend and I found the source. Evidently twelve years ago, when the house was built, a wallboard nail pierced (ruptured) the water line. Amazingly, the penetration somehow "self-sealed" and had remained so for twelve years. But with time, the water flowing through the line rusted off the end segment of the nail sticking into the pipe. Finally, the nail tip had fallen off, and water was spraying from the built-up pressure all over the wall—and it had soaked through and run down the hall wall. Tiny, small ruptures are ruptures just the same. And with time, the small fracture becomes bigger, and worse, when not corrected

Yet again, when living in Charlotte, North Carolina, we were blessed—and challenged—with the first opportunity of building a home from scratch. (If you've ever built a home, you surely understand what I mean by the "challenge" part of it!) A builder-developer in our church was offering us the deal of a lifetime to build in one of his new developments in an exploding part of town. We were beyond excited! Everything would be the way we wanted it because we were making all the choices, not inheriting someone else's.

As we watched it come out of the ground, we were so excited that I sometimes thought we were probably spending more time there than the construction crews. The framing, the exterior and interior walls, the roof, not to mention details such as the cabinet hardware, the floor coverings, wallpapers, paint colors—decisions,

decisions, decisions. Every one made as though it were equivalent to nuclear disarmament.

Imagine how thrilled we were when we moved in with our three kids. It was *ours*! We had built our dream home. And month by month we loved it more and more. Until the toilets wouldn't flush.

Nothing could be more of a wake-up call.

The plumbers were called. Which then brought the builder. Which ultimately required the city.

A rupture had somehow occurred in the sewer line. No wonder that one area of the front yard was greener than all the rest! But the rupture had created a stinky mess—literally! And until the house line was connected to the sewer line once again, we were up the proverbial creek.

All three memories drive home the fact that ruptures are bad news. And they need focused attention and action.

. . . .

RUPTURES DON'T JUST GO AWAY

All three challenges were different, and yet similar. Sort of like ruptures in relationships.

Each of them required intentional focus, a lot of work and tenacity until repaired. Exactly like ruptured relationships.

And each one of them occurred from different types of causes, much like wounds that occur in relationships—and especially in Father Wounds.

- The first was due to life pressures, demands, schedules, and expectations, and the resultant "rush" to get things done and the feeling of "I can handle all this pressure!"
- The second was fully unintentional. Seemingly tiny and insignificant. No big deal. Not even an awareness that it

had happened. But a little puncture became a significant break over time.

- The third was "hidden" by seemingly good signs on the surface (plenty of green grass), no thought that something could be wrong when so much "money and time" had been put into it. So, you can imagine the feeling of "this shouldn't be happening to us" that flooded into our lives.

Relational ruptures are so similar. Father Wounds happen equally unexpectedly. Demands at work, everybody's expectations, and the hectic schedules of family with kids involved in seemingly endless activities can all be the background of a dad saying (or not saying) something that leaves a wound. A dad, stepdad, or father figure who makes an unintended off-the-cuff statement—or who doesn't attend a child's event, thinking, "It really isn't that big of a deal anyway," or who is physically home but not engaged emotionally—leaves a wound that with time grows to resentment, anger, bitterness, or worse.

And since they don't just go away, dads, stepdads, and father figures need to discipline themselves to develop a sensitivity to what may be developing beneath the surface. We will need to be on the lookout for signs of rupture. It will help to review the following at the end of the day:

- Did we do—or not do—anything that could be the source of a wound?
- Did we say something we shouldn't have or not take the opportunity to express what we should have?
- Was there something we should have been at for our child because it was very important to them, even though it wasn't quite that important to us?

Perhaps one of the greatest end-of day reviews is to go right to the source—our kids. My friend Andy Stanley said several years ago that he tried to make it a regular practice while his kids were growing up to ask them these questions at the end of the day:

- Did anyone break a promise to you today?
- Did anyone let you down today?

We dads would probably create far fewer Father Wounds if questions like those had been taught in "Father School" (if only there were such a thing!). There's nothing guaranteed about such questions, but they show an intentional effort for preventive action of what can inevitably cause so much damage.

So, if ruptures don't just go away or repair themselves, what is the key?

At the center core of repairing and restoring ruptured relationships, such as Father Wounds, is *forgiveness*. So, let's take a look in the next chapter at what biblical forgiveness is and isn't, how God, our heavenly Father models it, and what it takes to practice it when we have been wounded.

NOTES

9 The Miracle of Forgiveness

WHERE FATHER WOUNDS exist, forgiveness is essential—for *your* sake, as well as for everyone around you and those who will follow in your footsteps.

Wounds leave ragged edges of hurt, offense, anger, and bitterness. All of these bring forth "infection" that eats away at relationships, contentment, and satisfaction in life.

William McKinley, who served seven terms in the U.S. House of Representatives as well as two terms as Ohio's governor, became the twenty-fifth president of the United States by defeating William Jennings Bryan. He would defeat his opponent by the largest popular margin since the Civil War.

Big business enjoyed unprecedented growth during his administration. He used the protective tariff as a way of shielding U.S. business and labor from foreign competition, and he successfully promoted the gold standard of currency. But he became known best for his foreign policy across the globe.

When the popular McKinley won a second term by an even greater margin over Bryan, it appeared he was on his way to an overwhelmingly second term. But on September 6, 1901, that expectation came to a shattered end. While standing in a receiving line at the Pan-American Exposition in Buffalo, New York, McKinley was approached by a Polish-American anarchist who, unknown to the president, was carrying a concealed .32 revolver in a handkerchief.

McKinley was shot twice at close range. One bullet deflected off a suit button, but the other entered his stomach, passed through the kidneys, and lodged in his back. Doctors frantically searched and probed for the bullet but failed to find it. As a result of the repeated probing and searching, as well as false assumptions that the president was "improving," the unseen enemy—now termed *gangrene*—soon spread throughout his body. McKinley died eight days later.

Take note: it was not the original wound alone that led to his demise but the infection because of the wound over time and the "revisiting" of it. Tragically, Thomas Edison had provided a brand-new X-ray machine to aid in "seeing where the human eye cannot," yet it was never used!

So it is with Father Wounds. The initial wound is hurtful, but it is the hurt, anger, resentment, and bitterness over time that becomes deadly to relationships.

. . . .

THE INEVITABLE CONNECTION

Relational wounds are like that. They always begin with a "wound," whether intentional or unintentional. A "wrong" is committed, at least in the eyes of the one wronged. The wound most often breeds a sense of rejection. That rejection, reflected upon (probed and played over and over in the wounded person's mind over time) in the wounded person's mind becomes more and more "infected." And that creates anger. And anger, over time, breeds an unforgiving spirit, which leads to the onset of bitterness.

WOUND   REJECTION   ANGER   UNFORGIVING SPIRIT   BITTERNESS

And the Scripture warns that bitterness, when it takes root, affects everything and everyone around the person holding it.

Remember, wounds don't always take place intentionally. They can be delivered by an off-the-cuff insensitive remark. I recall well Dr. Charles Stanley writing of an unintended Father Wound he didn't even realize he had caused when his son Andy was growing up. He recounted how Andy loved music and was always pounding on the piano, playing mostly by ear. There was little melody, just continuous crashing chords—over, and over, and over.

Sticking his head in the room one day he said, "Is that all you know, Andy?" Six words. It doesn't take more than three seconds to say them. But they caused a wound that was carried for years. Andy didn't play again when dad was home. That area and others became distant, according to Charles. And it wasn't until years later that Andy admitted that the wound created a sense of rejection that led to years of anger and resentment. What Andy had heard in his receiving of the message was more like, "I don't like your music, and for that matter, you, for playing that music." Interesting how wounds can be the result of one thing meant in the giving of a message and a totally different thing received from the message!

So, if forgiveness is to be extended, where do we start? And how do we get there?

· ·

WHAT FORGIVENESS ISN'T, AND WHAT IT IS

Let's start with a biblical definition of the meaning of *forgiveness*.

But before we get there, let's take a look at what biblical forgiveness is not. Many confuse forgiveness with other actions that are not synonymous in any way.

What forgiveness is *not*:

Toleration—taking the attitude that you will "put up" with a person who has hurt or wounded you. Forgiveness is not "putting up" with someone or "grinning and bearing it," plastering a fake smile on your face when the person comes into your presence. This can be the position a child takes with a father or stepdad who has wounded them just to keep the peace, or not to ruffle the family waters.

The tragedy with this approach is the superficiality of it. Nothing is changed in the internal area of life. Everything remains on the surface. Attitudes, emotions, and memories don't get addressed.

Meanwhile, the wounded person continues to convince himself or herself that they have handled the problem. "I don't have an issue with _____," they say. "I'm over it. It's old history."

Meanwhile the wound just goes deeper and becomes more "infected."

Repression/sublimation of the pain—just burying the past wound and trusting it will stay there. Playing mind games and pretending that something will stay buried doesn't work. The wound always resurrects! Keep it buried for a period, but wounds will retain their "life." They will actually grow with time. And they will often resurrect at the most inconvenient and awkward moments.

Yet we often pride ourselves for "keeping a lid" on it. We tell ourselves that we've gone the extra mile and that we haven't let it affect anyone else. What we don't see is what is happening inside of us as the pressure builds like a pressure cooker.

Oh yes, and when they erupt to the surface, the wounds, repressed feelings, hurts, and anger will inevitably and unimaginably be worse, more volatile, and the source of "collateral damage."

Minimization—This is the approach that causes the wounded to try to convince themselves that the wound "is no big deal." By this rationalization it is felt that by convincing oneself that the issue is "minimal," it will make the hurt go away. Men are especially vulnerable here. The male species has often been schooled in our culture that men "suck it up" and that "big boys don't cry." That is, males are not to show emotion.

But just because it is made to sound like a minor issue, either verbally or in one's mind, why is it that the sphincter muscle tightens when the *wounder* comes into the picture?

All of these fall far short of biblical *forgiveness*. So what does the Bible mean when it speaks of forgiveness? It means this:

> *Canceling the debt of a legitimate or perceived wound from another, restoring a view of worth to the offender, and ceasing to withhold the possibility of restored relationship*

Let's take just a moment and break that down into bite-size pieces:

Canceling the debt—This means ceasing to hold the other party responsible for having to do something in order to merit forgiveness; in other words, it means not requiring the other person to "owe" something in order to "earn" forgiveness, even an apology. Forgiveness can be granted, even in the face of a missing apology.

A legitimate or perceived wound from another—Sometimes wounds actually happen and they are obvious, but at other times they are perceived by the one who *feels* wounded by an action or inaction, words or attitudes of another. Even if it is perceived, it is still real to the one feeling it.

Restoring a view of worth to the offender—In order to fully and freely forgive, the forgiving party needs to see the "offending party" as still a person of worth who is created in the image of God.

Ceasing to withhold the possibility of restored relationship—forgiveness and restoration can be treated at times like a bargaining chip, temptingly held out, only to be snatched back, or simply held until the "debt" is finally "paid."

To see this truth personified, there is no better place to look than to God, the heavenly Father.

. . . .

GOD SETS THE EXAMPLE

To get a solid and clear view of forgiveness, we need to start with its ultimate foundation—and that's God. Let's take a look at how the heart of God was wounded and how He responded, and that will require us to take a look back to the beginning.

The Bible records that when God created Adam and Eve, He placed within them the *Imago Dei*, the image of God. They were given a body, a soul (emotion, will, and intellect), and spirit. With these qualities they would have the opportunity to have and experience an intimate, growing relationship with their Creator and heavenly Father. It would be the opportunity to not simply know about God but to, in fact, encounter Him.

With that came amazing provision, opportunity, and freedom. The most perfect environment ever to exist was to be their home turf. They would find every need and want provided for. Their opportunity would be boundless. God gave them dominion of His entire creation. Their freedom would be almost limitless. Coming and going would be at their discretion. It would be their decision as to what each of God's creation would be called.

Yet, there was only one loving boundary. There would be one tree in the middle of the garden (the tree of the knowledge of good and evil) that would be *out of bounds*. And if they crossed the boundary, the consequence would be they would surely die, for death had not applied to their life previously. And that death would be death both spiritually in the person's spirit, which would separate them from their Creator, as well as death physically, which would ultimately bring a cessation to life itself.

So, the boundary was for their good and safe-keeping, not their deprivation.

But free will being what it is, and human nature's willingness to consider crossing established boundaries, the seemingly predictable happened (at least from today's hindsight). Temptation knocked on the door with unsettling questions and statements:

God was questioned   ("Did God really say . . .?")
God was refuted   ("God did not say . . .")
God was replaced   ("You will be like God . . .")

And when humans sinned (*missed the mark*) because of their trespass (*purposefully crossing the boundary*), separation from God entered into the human race. Death now came in more than one realm. Physical death would now ultimately limit the human life span, but a person's spiritual life died immediately. The only way it would ever be made alive to God again would require a miraculous intervention.

In our relative-focused world many struggle with the idea of an absolute standard, yet that doesn't remove its reality. And reality dictated that with the separation came a need of forgiveness and reconciliation (due to a ruptured relationship). Sin would have to be recognized, confessed, paid for, and forgiven.

To aid humankind in recognizing their sin, God would give the Law, capsulated in the Ten Commandments and the declaration "Love the Lord your God with all your heart and with all your soul and with all your strength" (Deuteronomy 6:5). When any of these were broken in action, attitude, or thought, the person had broken God's standard. As the New Testament would later spell out, if anyone stumbles at any one point of God's laws and boundaries, they are guilty of all (James 2:10).

Sound harsh? Unfair? Just think about daily life. If I see the speed limit is 45 miles per hour and I drive at 57 miles per hour, I have broken the law. Maybe not as badly as someone who has hit 100 miles per hour, but I'm still a lawbreaker. And not to the degree, perhaps, of someone who breaks in a house or commits a robbery—but still a lawbreaker. Isn't it interesting how we try to grade and categorize sin, primarily to excuse whatever it is that we personally have done?

And take a moment to look at Adam and Eve in Genesis 3 when they were caught ignoring God's loving boundary. Adam blamed Eve, Eve blamed the snake, and I'm sure the snake (Satan) was thinking overtime as to where he could point the finger, while he had already blamed God for "holding out the best" and "having meaningless rules"! And ever since, when we abandon God's loving boundaries, we often discover the temptation to blame Him for our troubles!

Think a moment how God's heart had to be broken. The ultimate of His creation—those on which He had bestowed such freedom, love, and relational wealth—had suddenly turned their backs on their Creator and heavenly Father simply because they chafed against the boundaries established for their own protection and well-being. And having breached the relationship, they then immediately began to scramble to cover up their action. Sound familiar?

And yet God immediately began to move toward forgiveness by providing a temporary covering. In supplying covering, obviously made from an innocent sacrificed animal, so began the long movement of a loving God to restore a ruptured relationship. The problem was not with God but with man's heart. "The heart is deceitful above all things" (Jeremiah 17:9). And with that being the case, humans would come to the realization that their "iniquities have separated [them] from . . . God" (Isaiah 59:2).

History would evolve to show the ongoing effects of the ruptured relationship. Humans would continue to break God's loving boundaries and laws, and God would continue to act in forgiveness (though that did not always negate the consequences). As the people of Israel wandered through the wilderness, God would give them a reminder of His provision and His ways, commandments, and boundaries—which the Israelites would tend to take for granted and break or breach. They would carry the ark of the covenant that represented the mercy seat of God, where He would meet His people. Inside would be three representative items:

- The manna—representing both God's faithful provision, and humanity's rejection of it
- Aaron's rod—representing God's leadership, and humanity's rejection of it
- Tablets of the Law—representing God's holiness and standard, and humanity's rejection of it

And even during this period God was shouting how important forgiveness and repairing the ruptured relationship was to Him. He provided the Day of Atonement, where a lamb was provided as a covering for the nation's sin so that the relationship might be restored. But that was simply in line with what God had done all along.

- For Abel, God had accepted *a lamb for a man.*
- During the Passover God has accepted *a lamb for a family.*
- On the Day of Atonement God accepted *a lamb for a nation.*

And finally, in the first century, God would provide the ultimate payment for humanity's breaches of relationship with Him, "the Lamb of God, who takes away the sin of the world!" (John 1:29). Jesus Christ came to once for all pay the debt for sin—a debt he did not owe, yet a debt we could not pay. "Christ suffered for our sins once for all time. He never sinned, but he died for sinners to bring you safely home to God" (1 Peter 3:18 NLT).

From the beginning, God has been in the forgiveness business. Repairing the rupture of the relationship that His creation had caused became the focus of what is called "Redemption History"—the story of the Bible, from cover to cover. Allow me to close this chapter by just listing some of the great verses of the Bible that drive home the fact of God's passion for bringing together relationships that have been split asunder, and how He continues to love us even when we have not been loving:

> The LORD is compassionate and merciful, slow to get angry and filled with unfailing love. He will not constantly accuse us, not remain angry forever. He does not punish us for all our sins; he does not deal harshly with us, as we deserve. For his unfailing love toward those who fear him is as great as the height of the heavens above the earth. He has removed our sins as far from us as the east is from the west. (Psalm 103:8–12 NLT)

"I have loved you . . . with an everlasting love. With unfailing love I have drawn you to myself." (Jeremiah 31:3 NLT)

"I [the Lord] lavish unfailing love to a thousand generations. I forgive iniquity, rebellion, and sin." (Exodus 34:7 NLT)

"I—yes, I alone—will blot out your sins for my own sake and will never think of them again." (Isaiah 43:25 NLT)

Seek the Lord *while you can find him. Call on him how while he is near. Let the wicked change their ways and banish the very thought of doing wrong. Let them turn to the* Lord *that he may have mercy on them. Yes, turn to our God, for he will forgive generously.* (Isaiah 55:6–7 NLT)

Who is a God like you? Who forgives sin and pardons the rebellion of those who remain among his people? Who does not stay angry forever, but delights in showing loyal love? (Micah 7:18 NET)

In Christ God was reconciling the world to himself, not counting people's trespasses against them. (2 Corinthians 5:19 NET)

What an amazing God! He doesn't ask us to do what He has not consistently modeled. Think about it: He has consistently loved you and me and stood ready to forgive us at any moment, even when we were not lovable!

What an example of the power of forgiveness!

NOTES

10 God States His Expectation

S O WE'VE SEEN that God consistently and eternally stands ready to forgive, regardless of how badly He has been wounded by any of us.

But He also clearly states what He expects from us. That is critically important. One of the issues that causes so much damage in relationships, which we see repeatedly, is unmet expectations. It happens with couples, parents and kids, businesses, you name it. A core of that problem is that expectations are not clearly expressed and, therefore, not clearly understood. So no wonder relationships break down.

As we have seen, our God sets the example of loving forgiveness. The Scripture records repeatedly how He loves us right where we are, but too much to let us stay there. But He also clearly and straightforwardly sets forth His expectation so that, if nothing else, we can't claim we don't know what He is looking for from us.

Within a short time of enlisting His disciples Jesus gave arguably the greatest sermon ever given, the Sermon on the Mount. This was the clarifying of His worldview and that which He expected His followers to practice. In the heart of the message Jesus taught His followers a model for prayer (learning to talk with God, the heavenly Father). It was a pattern of key elements that effective prayer should incorporate.

Right in the middle of it we are jarred with the words "and forgive us our sins, as we have forgiven those who sin against us" (Matthew 6:12 NLT). Wait a minute! What did He say? That we should ask God to forgive us when we mess up *in exactly the same way we forgive others*! Could He really have meant that? Surely not!

That is exactly what He meant.

In fact, as though He thought we may have missed the message, He drove it home again two verses later when He said, "If you forgive those who sin against you, your heavenly Father will forgive you. But if you refuse to forgive others, your [heavenly] Father will not forgive your sins" (Matthew 6:14–15 NLT). Because He can't? Nope. He can do whatever He decides. But, if we aren't willing to grant forgiveness, we are also not ready to receive it!

GOD MAKES IT CRYSTAL CLEAR

God doesn't beat around the bush as to what He expects from us when a ruptured relationship exists. And nowhere is that more important than within the bounds of immediate family.

So, where Father Wounds exist, it is essential that we understand God's expectations of us. Regardless of the cause and source of the wound(s), God directs us to be initiators of the repairs. This does not mean that there will be no consequences from previous actions or inactions. It simply means that, for our sake, we are taking an essential step that can be a key to providing long-term healing. Without it, existing wounds *will not* simply go away with time. Time does not heal all wounds if the needed corrective steps are not taken. Without the critically important steps of repair, the infection simply goes deeper, lasts longer, and becomes more unmanageable.

Therefore, the question is, what are those steps?

God's answer is clarion clear:

> Be kind and compassionate to one another, forgiving each other, just as in Christ God forgave you. (Ephesians 4:32)

> Bear with each other and forgive one another if any of you has a grievance against someone. Forgive as the Lord forgave you. (Colossians 3:13)

"How is that possible?" you're probably thinking. It is only possible if the love that only God can grant to a heart is active. You may have been at a wedding in recent months and somewhere in the ceremony you heard 1 Corinthians 13 read. It is a beautiful passage and very popular at nuptials. But the problem is, it wasn't written primarily for weddings. It was crafted for daily living with those with whom we live life!

And it describes how God works in a person's heart to allow them to live in a supernatural manner. Just read it. No person living in their own strength could pull this off. Just review this:

> Love is patient, love is kind. It does not envy, it does not boast, it is not proud. It does not dishonor others, it is not self-seeking, it is not easily angered, it keeps no record of wrongs. Love does not delight in evil but rejoices with the truth. It always protects, always trusts, always hopes, always perseveres. (1 Corinthians 13:4–7)

Did you catch that? Love "keeps no record of wrongs." Does that mean that any hurt of the past is fully and completely forgotten? Probably not. Only God can completely and fully forget. Memories of experiences actually become chemically etched into the human mind. But it does allow for us to make the wise choice, and to be enabled to move forward, in health, for the future. Bondage to past experience and wounds can be healed. But to experience that, the right steps have to be taken.

Now you may be asking, "How many times do you have to forgive? I feel like I've done that before."

Peter was probably thinking something like that when he asked Jesus how many times he should forgive, and he threw out the number seven. Why? Because in that day the primary teaching by Jewish religious leaders was that to forgive three times was indeed "divine." So, with Peter adding four more times to that, it made him feel "super spiritual." Knowing Peter's charge-into-the-lead personality, he undoubtedly was waiting for his fellow disciples to call out kudos for his amazingly brilliant insight.

But Jesus brought him back down to reality by saying seven times was not enough; it needed to be seventy times seven! So was Jesus meaning 490 times? No, He was saying there shouldn't be a limit on our willingness to grant forgiveness. That it is one of the most critically important acts in life.

And is that only dealing with forgiveness of things that are easy, or at least not impossible, to forgive? Listen to C. S. Lewis as he addressed that critical question when he said, "To be a Christian means to forgive the inexcusable because God has forgiven the inexcusable in you."

"But I just don't know if I can do it," you're probably thinking. I understand that feeling. And the reality is, you probably can't. But God living in you can! But it will require you putting your pride aside. You can surely think of one hundred reasons why you shouldn't or couldn't. But that is your pride building the case. It will have to be set aside if a breakthrough is to occur. Martin

Luther summed it up powerfully when he said, "God creates out of nothing. Therefore, until a man is nothing, God can make nothing out of him."

Paul seemed to be saying much of the same thing when he instructed, "Be completely humble and gentle; be patient, bearing with one another in love. Make every effort to keep the unity of the Spirit through the bond of peace" (Ephesians 4:2–3). And Paul would say a hearty amen through his words in Romans 12:18: "If it is possible, as far as it depends on you, live at peace with everyone." That's our responsibility. But notice he doesn't stop there. He leaves room for God to deal with the issue when he says, "Do not take revenge . . . but leave room for God's wrath, for it is written: 'It is mine to avenge; I will repay,' says the Lord" (12:19).

God has an amazing way of dealing with issues that He feels need to be addressed, but it will always happen in His time and in His way. And we need to be okay with that. The fact is, He will handle it far better and more thoroughly than we ever could.

GOD ALSO GIVES A GENTLE WARNING

Have you ever found yourself constantly telling yourself, "Oh, I know I need to do that, and I'll get around to it—someday"? Or, "I understand I need to do that, but I'm just not ready yet."

Jesus addressed this procrastination in the greatest sermon of history, the Sermon on the Mount. Jesus challenged his followers:

> *"Therefore, if you are offering your gift at the altar and there remember that your brother or sister has something against you, leave your gift there in front of the altar. First go and be reconciled to them; then come and offer your gift." (Matthew 5:23–24)*

Let's put that in today's context. It is similar to saying, "If you are attending a worship service or a Bible study, or participating in a men's conference or small group, and you become aware in your thoughts of a ruptured relationship, you need to make it your priority to quickly go take the initiative to do whatever possible to repair the rupture."

And notice an interesting thing about this passage: it does not make a clear statement as to who is at fault, only that the relationship is ruptured and He expects His followers to take the initiative.

"But I don't feel like it, and besides . . . !"

It's so easy to make decisions based on feelings. "I don't feel like making the effort." "I don't feel they deserve forgiveness." "When I feel like it, I'll get around to it."

Feelings are not the rails upon which meaningful forgiveness usually runs. Feelings fail, while the will alone prevails. In order to get forgiveness done, the will must be in the lead.

Corrie ten Boom, who faced forgiving her Nazi persecutors and torturers, said it this way: "Forgiveness is an act of the will, and the will can function regardless of the temperature of the heart." So the key is not what I *feel like doing* or, for that matter, what I *don't feel like doing*. It all depends on what I decide and do as an act of my will, regardless of feelings!

"I'll forgive him when he . . ."

When it comes to Father Wounds, you may be thinking, "But he doesn't deserve it!"

Here's a question to ponder: When was the last time you deserved God's forgiveness?

And be careful about defaulting then to thoughts or statements such as "I'll forgive him when he _____." You fill in the blank.

Maybe it's ". . . when he says he was wrong." Or, ". . . when he asks for forgiveness." Yet again, ". . . when he admits to causing the hurt." Whatever the words are doesn't matter. They all indicate the same thing. You have created in your mind a *debt* that your father, stepfather, or father figure owes you. And until that debt is "paid," there won't be any forgiveness.

Remember the definition of biblical forgiveness from earlier in the book:

> *Canceling the debt of a legitimate or perceived wound from another, restoring a view of worth to the offender, and ceasing to withhold the possibility of restored relationship*

It means when it comes to a Father Wound, I can't put conditions on what the dad, stepdad, or father figure has to "pay off" in order to earn my forgiveness.

Take a moment and turn back to the end of chapter 2 where many of the causes of Father Wounds are listed as given by men from conferences. Which ones apply to you and your background? Are you holding on to a debt before you are willing to forgive? Why not make that decision today. It's not too late, regardless of the circumstances.

The ball is in your court.

NOTES

11 "What Do You Mean *Honor Your Father?* He Doesn't Deserve it!"

WHEN YOU HAVE experienced Father Wounds, where does the fifth commandment come into play?

If you can't immediately recite that one—or if you happen to not quite know the Ten Commandments in order—here is a helping hand. The fifth commandment reads this way: "Honor your father and your mother, so that you may live long in the land the Lord your God is giving you" (Exodus 20:12).

Okay, you're thinking, *If I had a dad that hadn't wounded me— hadn't hurt me repeatedly, hadn't left me feeling I was shortchanged as to his time, attention, and affirmation—it would be easy to honor him.* But how do you do that when your dad wasn't there? When he wasn't engaged? You're remembering the puts-downs, the not measuring up. The father's affirmation that was never regularly expressed.

Or worse yet, there may have been abuse. Or abandonment. Or alcohol or drug abuse. Or abuse of your mom in front of you, or at least with your awareness.

So, tell me, how do you honor that?

THE CRITICAL
JOURNEY OF GRIEF

When hurt and wounds have been present—perhaps even anger or bitterness—often a relationship has been ruptured at best, or lost at worst.

What was meant to be a wellspring of life has been shattered and seems at best difficult and at worst impossible to repair.

When such a loss happens in our relationships, what makes us think that grief doesn't apply to us?

Oh, that's just something that happens when tragedy strikes. When death occurs. When the bottom falls out.

But when Father Wounds have occurred, isn't it truly a tragedy? Doesn't something die within us? And compared to all our hopes and desires of how life should be, doesn't the "bottom fall out" of our expectations?

So, doesn't it make sense that we have to sufficiently grieve what we have missed through the heartbreak of Father Wounds?

REVIEWING
THE STAGES OF GRIEF

Those who deal with the medical arts are very familiar with the fact that grief has stages. The rest of us, not so much.

So, let's just take a moment and review what those stages are. But as we do, keep in mind that they are not necessarily linear (one stage doesn't always automatically follow after the previous stage like clockwork). So much will depend on the wiring of the individual, the circumstances on which the grief is based, and much more. But, in general, the stages are predictable.

Denial—This stage is filled with statements like "This can't be real!" "This couldn't/shouldn't happen to me!" "God wouldn't allow this, if He is so powerful!"

In Father Wounds, denial can take a very odd and unexpected turn. Some, not wanting to face the reality of wounds left because of disengagement, abandonment, neglect, or wounds of words or action simply make their father a "larger than life" figure in their mind and words. He did everything right. The failure of the marriage couldn't have been his fault. He wasn't there because he was so important and had a *big* job. And so, denial supplies the motive for avoidance.

Anger—This is where the raw nerve of wounds often surfaces for others to see. There is visible anger due to the dropped balls of the dad, stepdad, or father figure. The hurt causes life to get on edge, patience to become short or agitated, teeth to grind, and acid to churn in the digestive tract. And questions often fill this stage: "How could he have . . .?" "Why did he . . .?" "Didn't he know this would be the outcome?" "Why didn't he . . .?" "When will he admit he was wrong?" "What will it take for him to apologize?" "Will he ever make this right?" "How can he expect to have a welcoming place in the family after everything he did (or didn't do)?"

Bargaining—This begins to put conditions on the circumstances. And the bargaining can be aimed at the father, at God, or at someone else who should have stopped the circumstances that caused the wounds in their tracks. Perhaps a mom. A sibling.

And conditions begin to be placed on the table such as, "When he asks for forgiveness, then I'll . . ." "If he admits he was wrong, I may be willing to . . ." "If Mom would ever realize the role she played, then I . . ." "When my older brother or sister wakes up to . . ."

And of course, "When God makes it clear to me that . . . , then I will . . ."

Or at its worst, words or thoughts like, "God, if You love me and really care, then make my dad (stepdad or father figure) pay!"

Depression—It can be here that many get trapped. Things didn't work out like they hoped. Wounds were experienced. The other preceding stages may have all completely or partially occurred. And there is an emptiness or hurt deep in the soul of a ruptured or wounded relationship that should have been a great one.

After all, dad was to be the one who fulfilled each of the various critically important roles we looked at in chapter 6, but to be honest he totally flopped on one, two, or perhaps most of them. What could and should have been a great father-son relationship seems shipwrecked on the rocks of a dad's poor choices. And now there's no hope.

That's the core of depression—a feeling of hopelessness, when the person feels there is no way to fix it, to restore it, to revive it.

Acceptance—So, things that happened are what they are. But that is the past. Now the question becomes, "Is that where we are going to continue to live?" or "How can we repair this and make it what it should be going forward?"

While the past cannot be changed, it must be acknowledged and not denied, ignored, or minimized. Where there have been wounds, hurts, and disappointments, the only way to get beyond them with health for the future is to accept them for what they are but refuse to be crippled or trapped by them. This is the stage from which a person can move forward determined to become better from the past and refuse to become bitter.

Normally, where proper grieving does not occur, neither does healing. While not everyone grieves the same, it is essential that we acknowledge that we are wired to need its contribution to a productive and healthy future.

Lastly, especially where males are concerned, grieving is not something for "weak" people. In fact, one of the strongest things a man can do is to admit his need to deal with the past so that he may maximize the future.

BUT BACK TO THIS THING ABOUT HONORING YOUR FATHER!

You may be reading this and thinking of the fifth commandment of the Ten Commandments and responding in the following ways:

- *But you don't know what my father did (or didn't do)!*
- *How can I honor my dad (stepdad, father figure) when all I can remember is . . .?*
- *Had he earned being honored, I would be glad to honor him, but the fact is . . .*
- *Frankly, I know what the Bible says, but I don't feel like honoring him!*

Take a moment and recall that the commandment comes with a promise. After the first four commandments that deal with our relationship with God, God then moves to how we treat our parents as the first commandment of how we should treat those around us. The last six of the Ten Commandments deal with the horizontal plane of relationships in our lives, and God starts in the home.

Don't miss, too, that it is a commandment that carries a promise. God guarantees He will bless the one who *chooses* to honor his or her parent regardless of how they *feel* about the responsibility. What a great reminder that our decisions in life set a definite direction that will lead to an inevitable destination. And often, those decisions are a result of not primarily our *feelings* as much as an act of our *will*, regardless of our feelings.

God doesn't say, "Honor your father and mother because you feel like it, or because they deserve it." And He doesn't focus on the fact that it is primarily good for them when He states the commandment. Instead, God clearly declares that *you* will be the winner as a result, because it is the right thing to do.

SO WHAT DOES *HONOR* MEAN?

To *honor* means to treat with respect. So, does that mean you have to do it only if they are honorable and respectable? Look again. It does not include such a qualifier. Rather, it is a blanket statement. That also means it is not based on "feelings" such as warm and fuzzy memories. "Honoring" isn't just a feeling-based action but a willful decision. John Bisagno said it well: "The fifth commandment intends that we learn to honor because we need to learn to honor, not necessarily because our parents are worthy of that honor."[15] Interestingly, it is not primarily what it does for the parent that is central here but what it does for the child (young or grown) who does the honoring.

---

15 John Bisagno, *Positive Obedience* (Grand Rapids, Michigan: Zondervan Publishing, 1979), p. 37.

When the Hebrew Bible was translated to Greek the word chosen for *honor* was one used to signify honor surrendered to a superior and elder or that of a guest to a host. In the New Testament the same word would be used to designate "price" or "worth." So, honoring meant to *value* the one honored.

You may be struggling right now to think of anything worth honoring in your biological dad. But stop and think of this: he gave you life! And in a culture where abortion has long been "accepted" as a viable alternative, that you are alive is a major evidence that there is something there worth honoring.

The fifth commandment exists because it is in the home that honoring of all authority is learned. What is exercised there (in the home) will have effect as it is carried on at school, at work, on teams, and in relationships in general.

So, what will you choose?

As for me, I chose "honoring," and as a result, healing. But I came to realize that without me taking proactive, prescriptive steps it was not likely to happen. That is not to say that there is only "one way" or that "one size fits all." Life's circumstances may well have brought you in contact with a mature and wise Christian leader who can help you navigate the rough rapids of ruptured relationships to a safe harbor of healing. Or, you may know—or know of—a respected Christian counselor/therapist who you know has helped others with whom you are familiar find healing in repairing Father Wounds. By all means, seek that counsel and coaching.

One means that has helped many is a journey similar to what I took. In the pages following, Dr. Rick Fowler will share steps he has found helpful in helping many recover from Father Wounds in their own journey, and in many cases, repair them. I would hope that you would find these suggestions helpful. Remember above all else that there is no "silver bullet" that assures "just do this and the results are guaranteed." Healing ruptured or badly strained relationships is not a journey for the weak-hearted or for those who want "3 simple steps." Whatever the process, it will take sustained effort, a focused desire and undergirding prayer throughout the journey.

NOTES

12 Choosing to Recover– The Pathway to Peace (Some Helpful Coaching from Dr. Rick Fowler)

"I [God] will give you a new heart and put a new spirit in you; I will remove from you your heart of stone and give you a heart of flesh. And I will put my Spirit in you and move you to follow my decrees and be careful to keep my laws." (Ezekiel 36:26–27)

So far, this book has addressed how Father Wounds often persist even into adulthood. As the reader, you may now be asking, "Okay, I know I am still carrying around Father Wound baggage, so how do I get rid of it? I want to move on. Where and how do I start?"

To answer this question, the journey toward freedom and the healing of your Father Wounds will be tackled in two parts. This chapter will focus on your part, and in the next chapter, the emphasis will be on God's part.

Of course, in God's sovereign power, He could snap His fingers and immediately rid you of all the negative baggage you are now carrying around. However, in most cases He has us do our part, as He then comes alongside us and provides the victory. But in the process/journey we ourselves grow, change, and discover release and freedom. For example, God could have annihilated the enemies of Israel with the sound of His voice, but instead He had His chosen people prepared for battle and then encountered the enemy before God stepped in and ensured the victory. He told them that He would drive their enemies out "little by little" as He knew they would not be able to deal well with sudden change and total victory; nor would their needed strength for their future be built. The process would be step-by-step.

A truth for all people, everywhere, and for all times is *We cannot do what God alone can do, but God will not do what we ourselves must do.*

So, what is your part in gaining victory over your Father Wounds? Let's start by asking a question: *How much of a priority is it for you to be free from your Father Wounds?* I ask that question because many like to play the *victim* game. Or another way I could phrase this question is, *What price are you willing to pay to climb out of the ditch of frustration, or even destruction, over what happened to you?* Sadly, the fear of confronting a father is often unnerving, and sometimes boldness stops when it comes down to the final steps of truly resolving these issues in our lives.

Resolving the hurt you have experienced is not a one-shot exercise. Take the potential weight lifter for example. At the present he can only bench press 100 pounds, but his goal is to press 300 pounds. The athlete does not start out trying to immediately jump to lift 300 pounds, but rather he adds to the weights in small increments until he finally reaches the ultimate goal.

The journey to being healed begins with just you, God, and a pen and paper.

You may be thinking, "Wait a minute. I'm not into introspection and touchy-feely remembering. And I'm not a writer. This sounds corny to me."

Before you go any further, let me tell you (with his permission) that Bob had to do this with the Father Wounds he had experienced in his own life. So, this is not a theory or something that just sounds good but a very practical exercise to help you repair a very important area of life. And I've seen this prove to be fruitful in the lives of hundreds—many of them being men.

There will, most likely, be some emotions and memories that will erupt during this experience. Be ready to face them you as you revisit the pain and sadness of your past:

1. You may question, "Is it worth it to go through this ordeal?" "Is the pain greater than the gain?"
2. You may conclude that it is easier to avoid your dad, or the problem you have with him, rather than to confront him.
3. You may project an unreasonable goal on the outcome. In many cases, there will be a desire to have a "daddy" again (or a "parent-to-child" relationship with your father); however, if he was emotionally unavailable in your growing up years, the best you can now have with him is an "adult-to-adult" connection. Perhaps this reality will have to be grieved thoroughly in order for resolution to occur.
4. Your emotional life may be stymied and detached as an adult due to Father Wounds you endured. Research has shown that if, for example, a boy of ten is emotionally wounded on a perpetual basis by his father, and those hurts have not been resolved, at age thirty, in that one area,

he will be "emotionally stuck" at age ten. For instance, if he felt rejected at age ten, he will still feel rejected at age thirty, while every other aspect of his development correlates with his chronological age.

5. You can expect a surge of anger to develop while you are on your journey to positive mental health. Don't worry; this is totally natural. Thoughts may surface such as, "Why should I forgive my dad when he ruined—or at least crippled—my childhood?" or, "I am angry that his actions still affect me today." I have seen many express feelings like, "I am angry you left Mom for another woman." Sometimes constant negative thoughts and feelings like this will lead to some sense of depression for the short term, as well.

6. The fear of rejection may reemerge. "I was rejected once by my father; I don't want to be rejected again."

7. You will experience your emotions swinging from one side to another. Keep in mind that "assertiveness" when dealing with detachment issues is often an underdeveloped skill. Usually the emotion of either denial ("Oh, everything is okay") or extreme anger and outrage surfaces when a trigger situation emerges. For example, a thirty-year-old man rages when a car cuts him off—a sign of not being in control—because dad never let him control much of anything as he grew up. The origin of this rage may actually stem from experiences he had as a boy when he felt powerless when dealing with his father.

8. Expect different reactions from your siblings about Father Wounds. This may be a result of your siblings not experiencing what you went through. Or, due to their temperament being different than yours, everything is now fine in their perspective. Or, perhaps they never realized it happened at all as you were growing up together.

9. Hopefully, the emotion of "I want to be whole" helps you to move from
   a. conditional love to nurturing love—conditional love is most often based on "performance," and that is a ruthless standard for anyone to have to live by;
   b. self-disrespect to self-respect;
   c. emotional intolerance to emotional freedom;
   d. self-ridicule to encouragement;
   e. dogmatism to grace;
   f. denial of the importance of your inner life to encouragement and nourishing of your inner life;
   g. social dysfunction to social connection. (Social dysfunction is when a son who experiences abuse of any type by a father sees it as "normal" or "how all people are"; all other relationships are then viewed through this warped lens. True freedom comes only when a mental shift is able to be made to a new paradigm in which the abused person can now interact on an intimate level with others without the fear of rejection or shame—thus, social connection.)

Allow us to assure you that yes, it is worth the pain to obtain the gain—the victory in your emotional, physical, and spiritual well-being!

Now, with the above as a foundation, let's get to work, step-by-step.

. . . .

STEP ONE: WRITING DOWN YOUR STORY

The first step to recovery is to take 3x5 cards and on each, write down a memory, an emotion, or an event that happened in your growing up years. What you write down can be either positive or negative. Give yourself several weeks to download your past.

So, whenever a memory comes to mind, write it down. Also ask God to reveal anything that needs to be exposed. Remember, we can stuff those unpleasant memories deep into our subconscious. "Stuffing" doesn't mean they are not there; it only means that they are "stuffed," often awaiting the right set of circumstances to burst forth again, often to be used as a weapon.

Once that has been completed, sort the cards by your age at the time when events occurred and/or the emotions you felt and experienced, and begin writing your story. These specific events and memories can be used to craft a letter to be shared at the right time with your dad, stepdad, or father figure, or to use as a step-by-step guide as you talk to him in the future person-to-person.

Let's assume you are going to craft a letter that is meant to explain to your dad, stepdad, or father figure your hurt from the Father Wounds of the past as well as your heartfelt desire to re-store, revitalize, and renew the relationship for the future. *(NOTE, ADDENDUM 1 IN THE APPENDIX CONTAINS SAMPLE LETTERS OF CLIENTS WHO HAVE COMPLETED THIS EXERCISE AND MAY SERVE AS A HELPFUL TEMPLATE AS YOU CRAFT YOURS.)*

Part 1: Introduction

A sample beginning to your story might be, "Dad, over the past several months I have done a lot of soul searching and intro-spection about my growing-up years. As I contemplated incidents in my past, and how I now react to them in the present, I feel the need to share them with you." Yet another example of an introduc-tion might be, "Dad, when I couldn't make it home for Christmas due to the weather, I felt somehow relieved, honestly. To discover the reasons for that feeling, some important items emerged in my mind as I looked back through my memory bank that I need to share with you."

Part 2: Statement of Affirmation

Next, in your story to your dad, begin with several affirmation statements. Even negligent dads have done some things right! So, you might start off this way. "Dad, growing up I did appreciate your provision for the family, your hard work, and _____. So, thank you." Be genuine and sincere. Don't merely say something to check off the "affirmation" box. If you can think of several things for which you are thankful, it will help create an environment of openness and receptivity when you actually share them.

Part 3: Statement of Purpose

It is critically important to let him know that your focus is on specific items and circumstances, and not a condemnation of his total being. You might state something like, "Dad, the purpose of this letter is not to throw you under the bus but to share with you some memories of my growing up years that I have tried to bury but was unable to do so. I believe these negative memories have affected not only me but our relationship as a whole. I feel it is time to address my feelings and hopefully repair and reconcile my relationship with you."

Part 4: Addressing Specific Father Wounds

Sharing Father Wounds using bullet points seems to get better results. Men like specifics, not generalities. Don't use generalization words like *all* or *never* in your dialogue, but rather try something like, "I can remember on my twelfth birthday that you cussed me out in front of my friends, and I had to leave the table crying." Before listing how your father was emotionally abusive, I would suggest that you write in this section something like the following: "Dad, I may be right, or I may be wrong, but what I am going to share with you is how I really feel. If I am right, I would like to find positive ways to resolve the hurt I have experienced, and if I am wrong, I would like to know what caused me to feel that way." By expressing that type of statement, you have a comeback if your father says, "What you just said did not happen that way." You may then respond with vulnerable wording such as, "Dad, I might be wrong, so let's now explore why I came to that conclusion."

Each memory you listed on your 3x5 cards that you feel has contributed to the Father Wounds should be enumerated in similar fashion. Don't leave any important circumstances out. At the same time, be reasonable and don't try to see how big the list can become. Remember, the goal is clearing the air with open and vulnerable communication that can lead to repair and, hopefully, reconciliation of a relationship. It is not intended to air every frustration you have ever experienced.

Part 5: Desired Outcome

Now that you are an adult, state your desired outcome from this confrontation with your dad as an adult. Be realistic, not idealistic. This section may include a statement like, "Dad, my desire is to have a positive relationship with you. But for this to happen, the following boundaries must be in place so I can feel safe to be in (the relationship) your presence." Again, be specific and realistic with your desired goals, especially since you cannot start over as a child with your dad.

Part 6: Reaffirmation

In your story, you started with affirmation. At Part 6, you end with affirmation. A sample conclusion might look like, "Dad, I love you and desire a healthy relationship with you. Consider what I have written. My purpose in telling you my story was not to immerse you in guilt but rather to correct the wrongs of the past by establishing new relational ground rules that will benefit both of us moving forward."

. . . .

STEP 2: SHARING MY STORY WITH DAD

Based on your unique story, how you share your story with your father, stepfather, or father figure will depend on several factors that include the following:

A. Is your father deceased or unable to respond to your story?
Your Response:
If your father is not able to hear your story, I would suggest you use the *empty chair technique*. In this case, get a picture of your father and place it on the empty chair. Then share your story/letter as if your father were actually present—because in your mind and emotions he is. Disclose everything you wrote in the letter that has hurt you.

Then, by a volitional act of your will, *choose to extend forgiveness once and for all.* Feelings will not "lead the way" for this decision and act; feelings will follow when this decision is made and action is taken!

Choose to release the person from any debt that you have felt they owe you (as discussed in the chapter on forgiveness) and *say it out loud.* When this is done, thank God for giving you the grace to do so and for the healing He alone can bring.

This exercise may seem hokey to some, but there is much research data that suggests one can get positive emotional relief from doing this.

This is what Bob had to do since, sadly, his father died about twenty-four months before Bob was ready to do this activity. So, he actually got two chairs and sat them facing each other. He sat in one and imagined his dad in the other. And then Bob spoke out loud as though his dad were actually sitting in the opposite chair. While he admits it initially felt strange, he says today that the more he followed through, the more natural it became and the more he realized it was helping him.

As you consider this exercise, it is an important thing to remember that this is not for your dad, primarily, but *for you!*

B. Does your father feel there is not a problem? If so, he may be confused or even shocked to hear of negative memories from your childhood.

Your Response:

Often a father who has psychologically wounded his child will suppress his recollection or actually be totally ignorant of the harm of his behavior. Many fathers simply did what they experienced in their own dad-son relationship and may well not have understood the hurt they caused. Or, if they did, they may well have rationalized it away and "stuffed" its memory. Repression is one way he has learned to cope with the fact that he was not there for you in whatever way applies in your case. If your dad says, "Those things you are saying did not happen," use a technique called the *broken record technique*, which is basically to acknowledge what he says but then go back to your original statement and repeat it over again. For example, "Dad, I understand that you do not think "x" and "y" happened, but as I said a moment ago, it did occur at this occasion. And whether you realized it or not, this is how I felt."

A key point to remember is that one who has repressed the truth of an event or behavior will often try to change the subject. Don't take the bait. Words such as "Dad, we can talk about 'x' later, but now we are talking about 'y,' so let's stay focused on that" can be very useful here. Don't allow your focus to be derailed.

C. Do you anticipate that your father will become very angry over reading your story and play the role of the victim?

Your Response:

Your dad showing anger or victimhood is probably a trait he has used over the years in order to control you and others. However, now that you are an adult, you must see your dad as an equal and politely but firmly refuse to let him use these responses to gain control. One interesting observation is that woundedness often stems from abusive parents who see their children as threats and treat them accordingly. For instance, a dad can express anger toward a son for not doing something "right" fast enough, not "performing" to his expectations, or generally "not measuring up." By no means always, but more than once in a while, a dad's anger may be a result of his own insecurity.

It is important to remember that when a child is very young, the father can control his son at will through sheer power and fear. But as his child grows and begins to have a will of his own, his father may begin to see him as a threat (or at least a competitor for the "alpha role" in the family). At this stage, the father abuse often escalates in order to maintain dominance and control over his son.

Finally, if his anger is relentless, you may have to say to him, "Dad, I will not spar with you. I am postponing our discussion until you can listen and respond more calmly." When involved with an angry person, the rule of thumb is *never debate anyone when the emotions are high, and if the other person's voice goes up, yours needs to go down.* Remember, emotions and logic are like oil and water; they don't mix well. So, if you are trying to be logical, honest, and practical and your dad flies off emotionally, a delay in timing may well be in order in addressing the needed issues.

D. Are you aware of your part in the dysfunction between you and your dad?

Your Response:

In any conflict between two people, a vast majority of the time it is never 100 percent the fault of one person. It may be 80–20 percent or 60–40 percent, but in most cases, both parties are to take responsibility for their part. It is very likely that when you confront your father, he will bring up your faults to counter your arguments and attempt to shift the focus of the conversation back to you. At this point expressing your future openness can help defuse emotions through words such as, "Dad, I would love for you go through this same exercise and I will gladly listen to your side of the story. But today, I will only talk about what I have written, because my goal is to have a healthy and loving adult relationship with you."

* *

STEP 3: RESOLUTION OR RESIGNATION

This step can take a path in one of two very different directions. You must be ready to face either outcome. Because we live in a fallen and sinful world, not every conflict ends in a "happily ever after" scenario. If the outcome with your dad is not resolved, then resignation becomes the only option. I counseled one man whose dad refused to reconcile, and my advice to him was to keep appropriate boundaries yet pray for him every day. The dad would not talk to his son for over a year (aloofness is often an attempt to see if one will revert to the dysfunctional relationship of the past), yet a breakthrough came when his dad encountered health problems. His son, keeping healthy boundaries, was finally able to reconnect with his father in a positive way amidst the father's struggles and trials. But had the father never reconciled, the attempt made by the son to establish a healthy relationship with his father allowed him to move forward into a principle based on based on 2 Timothy 1:12, which paraphrased is "What you can't control, let go, and let God take over."

Before I move on, I mentioned that my advice to my client was to establish healthy boundaries. The following keys may help you in setting up healthy boundaries when they are needed:

A. **Establish healthy spiritual boundaries.** Recognize, accept, and live in the vital reality that your value comes from God, not from others. Your value is due to the *Imago Dei* (God's image), which He imparts into every life. Worth is not a performance-based asset. We must also accept God's grace when we, ourselves, make mistakes.

B. **Be honest with your feelings.** Honestly accepting, and acknowledging, our feelings gives us a tool to determine when our boundaries are violated. Feelings should never be our ultimate guide and counsel, but neither should they be ignored. They are often a helpful road mark for us to be perceptive and honest about what we are actually experiencing on a more subconscious level.

C. **Determine your needs.** When you determine and state your needs to your dad, you allow him to know your boundaries. This also allows you to take responsibility for your own actions, instead of waiting for him to tell you what you "should" do. By setting healthy boundaries, you will preserve your identity in relation to your dad. You will also gain self-respect that others cannot take away.

D. **In creating boundaries, remember it is acceptable, and often necessary, to say no.** A good point to keep in mind is this: if you feel uncomfortable saying no, you probably should!

The above is basically the worst-case outcome. Let's focus on the best-case scenario, where the father sees the error of his ways and genuinely wants to move forward with his son. If this reflects your situation, where to go from here may be unclear. Some advice. Always keep specific goals in mind at this step. People can say they are sorry, but if a new direction is not put in place, old habits will creep back in.

In a previous chapter, the topic of forgiveness—what it is and what it isn't—was presented. The takeaway we are to remember is that since God forgave us, we are to forgive others (your dad in this case). *Forgiving your father is your responsibility.* However, forgiveness and reconciliation are very different. In the worst-case scenario forgiveness is to be granted even though the father may have rejected it. And, because of that rejection, reconciliation was not possible. Reconciliation involves the cooperation of two individuals who have come together to resolve the hurts of the past. In the best-case scenario, this is what happens.

When people reconcile, they often say, "Okay, I will forgive and forget." Forgiveness does not erase the memory, but it allows you to move on without bitterness. My niece, for example, lost her arm in a car accident when her mother fell asleep at the wheel. It would have been understandable by some if she had become angry and bitter. "Mom shouldn't have been that tired!" "I paid the price for her not getting sleep!" "Why was she driving if she knew she was that tired?"

But my niece made some mature decisions. She chose not to drown in a blame game. Forgiveness and restoration occurred between mother and daughter. But does that take away the memory or the tragedy? No! My niece still wakes up every morning realizing she does not have a hand, but she has turned her handicap into a drive for success and is now a medical doctor. And mom and daughter have a great relationship.

You will never be able to erase the memory of your past hurts, but you can short-circuit that pain so its effects will not interfere with your daily life any longer. But it requires a choice of what you will allow in your thoughts and emotions, and what you will not allow. That, then, is the essence of reconciliation.

Regaining trust and safety with one who has abused you, betrayed you, or wounded you is a very difficult final step to take. Assuming you have forgiven your dad for the Father Wounds you have endured, and assuming he is also willing to reconcile, the last piece of the puzzle is the trust factor.

When a track star breaks his leg, the healing process begins immediately after the bones are reset and a cast is put in place over the injury. Then it takes six to eight weeks for the bones to heal, followed by several months of intentional, repetitive rehabilitation. The athlete then can begin to exercise by walking, jogging, and, eventually, running once again. One interesting point about healing: when the track star begins to run, his leg will feel pain as if the wound has not healed, so he must override the pain until he feels 100 percent again. So, in your case, you must realize that trusting your father again will take time so boundaries must be set (the cast) until the relationship is healed. And it won't happen in a Kumbaya moment or overnight. It will take time, and it can't be rushed.

Here is a helpful chart that may allow you to clearly distinguish between forgiveness, reconciliation, and trust:

FORGIVENESS	Focuses on the past	Only requires one person (you)
RECONCILIATION	Focuses on the present	Requires both people
TRUST	Focuses on the future	Takes time and must be earned

A FINAL WORD

Often in Scripture when *restoration* is discussed, a word is used that had medical implications. It referred to "the setting of broken, fractured bones." What a graphic picture. When relation-ships are ruptured and fractured, they, too, have ragged edges, splinters that have to be cleaned out and removed, and significant time is required—along with prescribed steps—to allow healing to occur.

But in relationships, when forgiveness is granted, spiritual help is usually required by mature and qualified people to complete a process toward *reconciliation* and *trust*. An atmosphere of support, encouragement, and integrity-filled motives is essential.

Author Lewis Smedes clearly outlines for us the vast differences between forgiveness and reconciliation/trust:

> *It takes one person to forgive.*
> *It takes two to be reunited.*
> *Forgiving happens inside the wounded person.*
> *Reunion happens in a relationship between people.*
> *We can forgive a person who never says he or she is sorry.*
> *We cannot be truly reunited unless the other person is honestly sorry.*
> *We can forgive even if we do not trust the person who wronged us once not to wrong us again.*
> *Reunion can happen only if we can trust the person who wronged us once not to wrong us again.*
> *Forgiving has no strings attached.*
> *Reunion has several strings attached.*[16]

If the above steps are too hard for you to accomplish on your own, may I suggest that you utilize the wise, spiritual counsel of a godly mentor or Christian therapist to help you in this journey of recovery. There is *nothing weak* or *unmanly* about doing so! In fact, it takes a strong man to admit he needs a helping hand in doing what is right.

---

16 Lewis B. Smedes, *The Art of Forgiving* (New York: Ballantine, 1996), p. 27.

This chapter has outlined your responsibility in the recovery process with your father. In the next chapter we will focus on what you can expect when you also engage God's help in the process of finding victory over your situation.

NOTES

13 Key Steps to Finding Closure
(Some Additional Helpful Coaching from Dr. Rick Fowler)

"I will repay you for the years the locusts have eaten . . . Then you will know . . . that I am the LORD your God, and that there is no other." (Joel 2:25, 27)

THE GREAT THEOLOGIAN A. W. Tozer once said, "Truth is like a bird with two wings. If you destroy one wing, the bird will not fly." Counseling, in a Christian environment, is like that bird with two wings, for it involves two inseparable, and mutually dependent, dimensions. One dimension focuses on what a client can do from a human perspective. The second dimension acknowledges that lasting victory over past wrongs and wounds cannot be obtained unless the inner soul is healed as well.

When counseling men who have been the recipients of Father Wounds, I often share my formula for victory:

1 (client's responsibility) + **1** (God's part) = **WON!**

I base this model on Philippians 4:13, which states, "I can do everything through Christ, who gives me strength" (NLT). In this verse we see the two dimensions of complete healing:

1. "I can do everything": my part
2. "through Christ": God's part

Men (and women) must realize that when working on getting over the mountain of childhood, adolescent, or young adult wounds, true and lasting healing only comes when you include the spiritual dimension that is revealed to us in God's sacred Word, the Bible. If you are trying to resolve your issues solely by human strategies and efforts apart from utilizing the second dimension of the formula, God's power, you will hit roadblocks that will keep you from getting over (let alone "soaring over") the obstacles you face. Listen to the promises of God, available to all who are willing to tap into His power source: Isaiah 40:29–31 states, "[God] gives strength to the weary and increases the power of the weak. Even youths grow tired and weary, and young men stumble and fall; but those who hope in the Lord will renew their strength. They will soar on wings like eagles; they will run and not grow weary, they will walk and not be faint."

For those of you who have been wounded by your father, stepdad, or father figure, I share the following story of a past client of mine whom we will call Bill. Even though he was a Christian, he did not initially tap into the second dimension of God's power plan, which resulted in many years of misery. The good news is that after intentionally bringing God into the equation and re-linquishing control to Him, he was able to begin releasing the shackles of his traumatized past and, finally, find true release and victory.

Allow me to open the door to Bill's journey:

Bill, age twenty-seven, came to my office for PTSD (post-trau-matic stress disorder) therapy. At age twelve he witnessed his father get into a violent argument with his mom and then shoot her. Though she survived, it took his mom over nine months for her wounds to heal from the ordeal. And Bill never did. Bill's father was sent to prison, and at the time of our sessions, Bill's father had just been released from incarceration and was seeking to regain a relationship with his son.

Some quotes Bill shared with me:

> "I can NEVER forgive him for what he did to Mom."
> "I couldn't care less if I never saw Mike (interesting, Bill used his father's name instead of "Dad") again."
> "I've been in turmoil for all these years; that day still haunts me."

Bill's mother told me he had accepted Christ as his Savior when he was ten years old. At that time, he was outgoing and very active in his youth group. But after the tragic incident he started to withdraw into a cocoon, bottling up his anger and hate for his father. Bill got married at age twenty-four but found himself being harsh with his wife when his "buttons" were pushed.

As a counselor, I realized that the root of his PTSD had dug deep into the soil of his mind and emotions, and the root had turned into a gigantic tree that bore the fruit of despair, anger, and depression. I told him that apart from coming to God for His healing power, he would not find victory for life, whether it involved forgiving and moving past his pain from childhood or being able to have genuine and close relationships with others as an adult.

So, my initial sessions with Bill focused not on the incident but rather on the spiritual battle that was raging inside him. Even though working through the trauma itself was important, I felt if he didn't open the cocoon and deal with his inner self first, he would never find full resolution on the issue with his father.

As I first turned my attention to the second dimension of therapy, I began to discuss with him what it means to "love the unlovable" and how Christ would want him to respond to the one who had wounded him so deeply (an impossible feat unless the issues are funneled through the second dimension of therapy!). We also discussed the prerequisites for reconciliation and the power of the genuine love that only the Holy Spirit gives us in the restoration process.

I shared with him that he should not fall into the trap of viewing his scenario from the human perspective—which focuses on rationalization (for example, since dad emotionally abused me, he deserves a good cussing out and anything else he gets from me). This, I told him, is like looking through a knot hole in the fence—it narrows perspective and would prevent him from seeing many of the implications of his decisions. Rather, he should attempt viewing the process of forgiveness from the spiritual perspective—so that he could then see the whole valley from the "mountaintop" of Scripture with clarity.

The power of love is an essential ingredient in healing a relationship. "Love," I told him, "must not be interpreted in terms of the humanistic definition that legitimizes behavior if it brings pleasure." Too often we get the idea that love is some warm, mushy feeling toward someone. But that kind of love fluctuates and is never constant. It is easily affected by moods, weather, blood sugar, recent circumstances, and so on. So, what is the love that God talks about us needing to have the ability to forgive and restore within relationships? The New Testament gives us the answer:

And this is love: that we walk in obedience to his commands. As you have heard from the beginning, his command is that you walk in love. (2 John 6)

Again, the Apostle John said, "But if anyone obeys his word, love for God is truly made complete in him. This is how we know we are in him: Whoever claims to live in him must live as Jesus did" (1 John 2:5-6). Similarly, the Apostle Paul wrote, "Love does not delight in evil but rejoices with the truth. It *always protects, always trusts, always hopes, always perseveres*" (1 Corinthians 13:6–7, emphasis added). It sounds so *nice* and *perfect*. How can anyone do that when they have been wounded?! Paul had already spoken about a key that much be present for that to ever occur when he said, "Love . . . does not demand its own way. It is not irritable, and it keeps no record of being wronged" (13:4–5).

I went on to impress upon Bill that love is the drive that desires the ultimate best for another (even his father, who had created wounds) within the guidelines of God's Word. This led to the reality that reconciliation cannot be genuine unless there is the love component in the formula. The word *reconciliation* in Scripture carries various shades of meaning. The Apostle Paul stated that due to Christ's work on the cross we have been reconciled with God (pardoned for our sins through Christ's satisfaction of the demands of God's justice and thus paying our debt to God) and thus brought back into relationship with Him (Ephesians 2:16). The word also implies forgiveness that takes place when repentance occurs. Remember, forgiveness can take place even when there is no repentance on the part of the other person. Forgiveness requires only one person and focuses on the past.

Reconciliation, on the other and, requires *both* people, and without repentance on the offending party's side the likelihood of reconciliation lasting is doubtful.

The key to Bill's reconciliation with his father included three facets:

1. Humility, which is essential to forgive
2. Forgiveness, which is necessary even without reconciliation
3. Acceptance that there may be times when we are forced to agree to disagree

Viewing our issues from a biblical dimension, then, is a realization that true healing grows out of true love—love that is committed to God's best for the offending individual.

Wow, that's tough! Especially when all we desire sometimes is for the person who wounded us to *pay a price*! But this doesn't mean that nothing can ever be said. Paul made it clear that sometimes there is the necessity of godly reproof (correction). But how reproof is done is key! That is why Paul clearly said we can reprove as long as we make sure we are "speaking the truth in love" (Ephesians 4:15). That doesn't mean what is said is "soft" or avoids reality. It does mean that what is said must not be driven by anger, revenge, or hurt that desires *to set the record straight* or to *get even while the getting is good*. What an important guard on our lips that guidance is!

I concluded this part of my counseling by giving Bill some practical steps he could take in speaking the truth in love to his father:

A. **Ask God for wisdom**—not only for guidance in what he should say to his father, but also wisdom as to the proper timing of the discussion. Many times, we confuse our preferences with biblical absolutes—God's wisdom will help us discern the difference.

B. **Beware of your attitudes**—I helped Bill realize that a holier-than-thou attitude would defeat his best intentions.

C. **Stick with facts and beware of throwing around feelings**—I encouraged him to stay in the "rational" versus the "irrational" during any confrontation.

D. **Be sure of your ultimate goal**—I told him to remember that true healing only grows out of true forgiving and an intentional determination to truly forgive his dad.

What ultimately changed Bill's worldview from revenge to compassion was completing two "second dimension" exercises. Only then could he begin the steps of recovery outlined in the previous chapters. They will lead you to literally write out your own story of hurt and wounds. I often suggest it take the form of a letter to your dad, stepdad, or father figure. As it is edited and refined over time you may simply use it as a guide in your discussion with a dad, stepdad, or father figure who lives close by or with whom you are visiting. If they are a long distance away, you may need to consider sending it to them by mail with a request to talk after they have read it. If they have passed away, this exercise of writing it out and using it in the *Empty Chair* exercise (discussed in the preceding chapter) will be important. This document will serve as your road map for a discussion and journey that must take place if healing is ever to occur.

I suggest you who are struggling with Father Wounds do the same. Here is how they work.

EXERCISE ONE: Establish a Spiritual Journal

1. I had Bill outline what specific emotion he was currently experiencing (e.g., anger, detachment from his father,

inner turmoil, etc.) in a blank journal. He could purchase a journal at an office supply store or stores such as Target or Walmart.

2. The next step was daily reading and meditating on any portion of Scripture. In Bill's case, he started by reading five minutes a day for a week and then added five minutes a day each week thereafter. (Usually, I have my clients start out reading from the Psalms and Proverbs as they so effectively get to the core issues of life and express the vast emotions we all go through when we are hurting).

3. At the end of each reading, I requested that he ask God to reveal to him at least one heavenly insight on one or more of the specific feelings he was experiencing and write those nuggets down in his journal. It is important to realize that some days it may be a struggle to write down even one insight on one emotion; then on other days, there may be several insights on numerous emotions that will be recorded.

4. Then once a week, he was to reread journal entries and again write down what God had revealed to him.

At first Bill resisted doing this because he was "mad at God" as well as his dad. So, I challenged him to commit to this assignment for just one month and to be open to God's working on his inner self. The first week, he barely wrote down a sentence, and his insights were very shallow. But then, an interesting thing happened. As the weeks progressed, he started writing in more detail, and I could see that the Holy Spirit was beginning to change his worldview regarding how he thought about his father.

EXERCISE 2: The Fruit of the Spirit Analysis

While he was working on exercise one, in his weekly visits we began to work on exercise two, which is based on Galatians

5:22–23. In this exercise, we took each fruit mentioned and related it to Bill's situation. The fruit depicts the qualities of Christ's life that are place in us, to be cultivated and grown, when we accept Christ as Savior.

It is helpful to use a measurement to identify intensity, so I said, "Bill, on a scale of one to ten, where ten indicates much fruit and one, little fruit, where are you when it comes to love?" Bill said, "One." "Okay, then," I said. "What would it take to get that one up to a two?" So, at each session, we would discuss a particular fruit and find ways for him to grow in that area. By analyzing each fruit of the Spirit, specific goals could be attained. In this way Bill now knows what to pray for concerning each issue he is facing.

We defined the fruit mentioned in Galatians and then applied those definitions to Bill's current life. A summary is as follows:

> **Love**—It is produced in the heart of the yielded believer by the Holy Spirit. Its chief ingredient is self-sacrifice for the benefit of the one loved. And it is *not* an emotion but rather a decision of the will.
>
> **Joy**—A state of being; an attitude (1 Thessalonians 1:6). This is fueled by gratitude and thanksgiving, leading to a sense of contentment. And it is not driven primarily by circumstances, but by attitude.
>
> **Peace**—Tranquility of mind based on the consciousness of a right relation with God and His resultant protection, care, and guidance, even in the midst of life's storms.
>
> **Patience**—Includes the idea of forbearance—patient endurance of wrong under ill-treatment without anger or thought of revenge.
>
> **Kindness**—A quality that should pervade and penetrate the whole nature. Being gracious to others in word, deed, and attitude and doing random acts of kindness.

Goodness—Refers to that quality in a person who is ruled by and aims at what is good—namely the quality of moral worth (Romans 15:14; Ephesians 5:9; 2 Thessalonians 1:11).

Faithfulness—An element produced in the life of a yielded Christian by the Holy Spirit, making the person persevere, endure, and continue under the most trying circumstances. I can remember hearing my dear friend Dr. Adrian Rogers regularly offer a cogent warning: "A faith that falters before the finish had a fatal flaw from the first."

Gentleness—Refers to quality of mildness in dealing with others.

Self-control—Having mastery or possessing power to control one's own desires and impulses.

Each week we summarized and evaluated Bill's progress. In this step Bill stated what he had learned about his problem from the completed biblical research he did each week. Four questions were repeatedly asked:

- What factors contributed to your progress this past week?
- What factors, if any, contributed to your regression?
- What biblical truths did you learn this past week concerning your problems?
- With God's help, what goals will you set for yourself this upcoming week?

I stated at the outset that Bill came to my office with PTSD and was stuck for years in the ugly memory of the incident that happened when he was twelve years old. By introducing him first to the second part of the formula, he then could tackle the demon that had plagued him for many years and *win*!

In solving the Father Wounds you have encountered, you must, of necessity, keep your eyes on the Mark, Jesus Christ Himself (see Philippians 3:14 KJV). Keeping your eyes on the Mark means you have turned 180 degrees around from your past way of interpreting life, allowing God to "restore to you the years that the locust [has] eaten" (Joel 2:25 KJV). As you develop and deepen your positive habit of prayer, reading God's Word and acting on it, spiritual fruit will grow, and the agony of the past will begin to diminish. Never forget that Christ is the Master Counselor and He is there to come alongside you at any of the following three levels of difficulty:

> **Level 1:** If your problem is a mere frustration, you are to *cast* your problem to the Lord (1 Peter 5:7).
>
> **Level 2:** If your problem proves to be heavier and more difficult, *roll* it onto the Lord (Psalm 37:5, "commit" in the original language means "to roll").
>
> **Level 3:** And, if your problem is too great for you, God promises to *take it off your shoulders* (Psalm 81:6).

Resolve this day to begin the process of restoration with your father. Your grandchildren will thank you for it.

NOTES

14 The Choice is Yours!

"So, where do I go from here?" you're probably thinking. Well, honestly, that's totally up to you.

Have you ever stopped to think that you are the sum of your choices?

Choices play a huge role in our lives.
They set a direction . . .
That leads to an inevitable destination (depending on the decision) . . .
That creates a destiny.

You've been challenged throughout the journey through this book to make decisions regarding what you are going to do about Father Wounds. Don't take that lightly. Your choices will make, or break, the future.

BUT I'M TRAPPED IN A GENERATIONAL CURSE ON OUR FAMILY

In our day, it has become popular to blame personal and family problems on some sort of generational curse. Often, scriptures referred to are Exodus 20:5; 34:7; Numbers 14:18; and Deuteronomy 5:9. The term is often thrown around as though it describes a journey that occurs when a father grievously sins, thus trapping his descendants to suffer resultant consequences for multiple generations.

My purpose here is not to get into the validity of generational curses, or their invalidity. It might be beneficial, however, to consider that the context of the Old Testament passages is idolatry, which was repeatedly a tripping point for the people of Israel. Israel was also the specific nation to which the warnings were addressed so we repeatedly see divine punishment meted out to Israel through disasters, destruction, and captivity.

But it is very clear in our day that choices do have consequences. And the consequences can affect many who had nothing to do with the decision. Therefore, without question, the effects of sin are passed down from one generation to another. When a dad or stepdad makes sinful choices and chooses sinful lifestyles, it often reveals itself in the next generation(s). Thus, when a father is an alcoholic, it often is seen that the struggle continues in the succeeding generations, as is abusive nature, uncontrolled anger, and so on.

What is essential to understand is that, ultimately, God holds each of us responsible for our own choices and actions. Listen to how He clarifies that in Ezekiel 18:2–4 (NLT):

> *"Why do you quote this proverb concerning the land of Israel:* *'The parents have eaten sour grapes, but their children's*

mouths pucker at the taste'? As surely as I live, says the Sovereign LORD, you will not quote this proverb anymore in Israel. For all people are mine to judge—both parents and children alike. And this is my rule: The person who sins is the one who will die."

If you continue to read Ezekiel 18, you will find that God even gives an example of a father who sins and then has a son who chooses to follow in his sinful patterns. God asks, "Should such a sinful person [the son] live? No! He must die and must take full blame" (18:13). In other words, he will be responsible for his own sin and choices.

But God then questions, "But suppose that sinful son, in turn, has a son who sees his father's wickedness and decides against that kind of life" (v. 14). Interesting scenario! The grandson has chosen to stop the slide of generational sin. He is planting his flag and saying, "Regardless of what has happened in my family's past, it stops here and now with me. I will choose not to repeat sinful patterns, and I will do everything possible to live a life that honors God, and which God can honor."

Of such a decision God says, "Such a person will not die because of his father's sins; he will surely live. But the father will die for his many sins—for being cruel, robbing people, and doing what was clearly wrong among his people" (v. 17b–18). So, generational sin patterns can be stopped!
To make sure that we got the clear message, listen as God's Word continues to clarify the issue:

"'What?' you ask. 'Doesn't the child pay for the parent's sins?' No! For if the child does what is just and right and keeps my decrees, that child will surely live. The person who sins is the one who will die. The child will not be punished for

the parent's sins, and the parent will not be punished for the child's sins. Righteous people will be rewarded for their own righteous behavior, and wicked people will be punished for their own wickedness. But if wicked people turn away from all their sins and begin to obey my decrees and do what is just and right, they will surely live and not die. All their past sins will be forgotten, and they will live because of the righteous things they have done." (18:19–22 NLT)

Talk about amazing grace! New beginnings! A fresh start! What a God!

Ponder this question: Have you ever noticed that God has far more to say about generational blessing and grace than He ever does about generational sin or curses? God far more desires to be the One who is faithful, loving, gracious, and the giver of blessings from generation to generation. It would seem to me that this is where we should focus. Everyone is responsible for their own sin will be held responsible accordingly by the Lord.

But at any point, change can happen! And it all centers, according to Scripture, in two steps:

1. Recognizing God's amazing grace, and your need of it, and repenting of anything and everything in the past that has been in disobedience to God and His will and His ways
2. Surrendering your life unapologetically and unashamedly to God, through Jesus Christ, His Son (Romans 12:1–2)

And the result is that when that happens, we become a brand-new creation. In 2 Corinthians 5:17 God promises that "if anyone is in Christ, the new creation has come: The old has gone, the new is here!" The word "new" in the verse doesn't mean "new in time," such as a piece of art, or a new house that was just finished.

Rather, it means "new in nature." The old nature is replaced by a brand-new one, thus a new start and fresh beginning is possible.

By the way, Ephesians 2:8–9 reminds us that this amazing and miraculous process is not dependent on something we do or steps we take in our own strength. From beginning to end it is a work of God's grace in us. It is dependent not primarily on what we do but on what God has already done!

. . . .

SO, YOU SAY YOU WANT A CHANGE

When I hear the term *dysfunctional family* I have to smile to a certain degree because I realize that every one of us is dysfunctional, and therefore, we are all in dysfunctional families to one degree or another. After all, all families are made up of people, right?

As I look back on my own family background, a bit of which I shared with you in chapter 5, I have to sit back and shake my head. When considering both my biological family and my adopted family I have had forebears who were alcoholics, relationally challenged, murderers, deceivers, given to fights, physically abusive, adulterers, cheaters, and manipulators. Thankfully, they were scattered among some very caring, upright, honest, and dependable people. There have been marriages that were solid (though they were few), marriages that ended tragically in divorce or betrayal, and those in which spouses simply coexisted.

So, when I launched out to start my own family, I found myself playing catch-up. I hadn't had a lot of firsthand models of how to build a strong family. My biological dad, as I shared earlier, was an alcoholic. My adopted dad was a strong provider but struggled with insecurity and relational baggage due to his horrendous upbringing. For instance, I don't ever remember seeing my dad hold my mom's hand. I never heard him pray. Being warm and affirming wasn't natural for him.

And suddenly, I found myself married!

I will always be thankful for my father-in-law, who was an outstanding model to me of how to treat a wife. How to be warm and affirming, yet a man's man at the same time. How to set boundaries and make clear the consequences. How to verbally build up and encourage, as I watched him especially with his wife and daughter (now my wife). That model was invaluable to me as a template of what leadership at home could and should be.

But as Cheryl and I began our marriage, I watched my dad and mom hold her at arm's length. Be critical. Use expressions that showed disapproval, regardless of what words were said. I realized that this is a way they had established of using manipulation to express disapproval throughout the years. And I had a decision to make. If I allowed this to go on, the inevitable outcome would be strain at best and alienation at worst.

So, I made the decision that it had to come to a stop with me setting a boundary that was clear and in which the potential consequences were understood. I arranged a time with my mom and dad, and, sitting down with them, I shared that I needed to address an issue that could not be ignored.

First, I expressed my deep appreciation for all they had done for me. Adopting me out of a heartbreaking set of circumstances, even when they didn't have a lot of resources or education. Giving me a home that was safe and had love (notice, I didn't say "perfect"). Providing for my needs, and numerous "wants," and allowing me to be the first in that family line to go to—and finish—college.

But I shared with them specifics in what I had observed in how they were treating Cheryl. I told them I couldn't speak to the motive as to whether it was intentional, but that it seemed to be.

Then came the hard part. I used words that went something like this:

> *I love you and am thankful for you. But I am heartbroken about what I am watching. I need you both to understand something very clearly. You need to stop these actions and attitudes immediately or there will inevitably be very sad steps I will have to take. I have chosen Cheryl as my wife, and I love her with all of my heart. We are working hard to make a new home that God can bless, and we will hopefully have children in the future who will be your grandchildren. And I hope that we will have days that will be filled with joy.*
>
> *But, for that to happen you will have to make a choice. The Bible says that when a man "cleaves" to his wife he must simultaneously "leave" his father and mother. That doesn't mean a cessation of relationship but that his primary allegiance, after his commitment to Christ, is his commitment to his wife.*
>
> *With that understanding, I hope you won't force me to make a choice between who I am going to have as the priority, at this stage, of my love and commitment. Hear me say that it will be Cheryl, if that choice is forced. I don't want there to be any doubt. And if that were to occur, the primary loser would be the two of you. I don't want that.*
>
> *So, you have a choice to make. You can embrace Cheryl as my wife and your daughter-in-law, and work to build that relationship, or you will experience what I just said.*
>
> *The ball is in your court and you have a decision to make.*

I then graciously excused myself and left the room, giving them time to talk between themselves.

Was it easy? No! Was it something I wanted to do? No! But was it something I needed to do to say this sinful tendency stops here and now? Absolutely.

Over the years I had watched my dad manipulate circumstances based on a reaction to his tragic upbringing. But I had also seen my mom do it, having learned the process from her mom, using emotions and looks to accomplish the same desired outcome. And I couldn't let that pass on to affect my marriage and family.

Was the response instantaneous and they ran to Cheryl and immediately asked for forgiveness and hugged her and everything was "happily ever after"? Hardly. But it did start a long, slow process that improved over time. It had its high points and numerous valleys, but the line had been put in the sand and the consequences were clear. And I had made a decision to stop unhealthy trends in their tracks.

Ironically, that journey helped prepare me for how I needed to handle the people my kids chose as mates, when the time came. I didn't always do everything perfectly, I'm sure. But I've tried to work hard to make my son-in-law and daughter-in-law feel welcome into our family and accepted and loved. They are the persons my daughter and son chose, and as result, it is my responsibility to receive them and support them and my kids in their choices.

- -

BUT WHAT ABOUT NEGATIVE PATTERNS BEING POTENTIALLY

PASSED ON TO YOUR OWN KIDS?

Did you ever find yourself saying, "Whatever happens, I'll never be like my dad in that area" or "When it comes my turn as an adult, I'll never do that" or "I'll sure do it differently"? Those words came out of my mouth more times than I can remember, as much as I loved and appreciated my adopted dad. Still, I had seen the consequences of his own Father Wounds and how they affected me and my adopted mom.

But guess what happened—as I got married and established my own family, I found that the impact of "passed-on baggage" can be astounding. And if not stopped, it can just keep on keeping on in the next generation. Allow me to vulnerably share a few examples.

Earlier in the book, I shared that my dad, through his own extremely dysfunctional childhood, grew into a man who worked hard to prove his love primarily through providing. Since he had never been provided for, I understand now, that he felt providing showed the ultimate height of his love. I just wanted him to be there—but too often he wasn't. He was off working in order to provide.

And then I became a father, as well as a husband. What a new experience. I had grown up primarily as an adopted child in an only child family. Now I found myself with a wife (who had a different background and set of expectations than I had) and three children—all of whom wanted and needed time. And what was I doing? Working hard to provide, sometimes being gone 32 to 33 weeks yearly on the road speaking, teaching, training, and building a career.

Cheryl would tell me later that her dad (remember, he would become a mentor and model in my life) seemed to always live with a base philosophy of "My family will get my best, and if I have to make a choice, the businesses will have to take back seat." But when we got married, and I began to exhibit repeatedly some of the very actions I had said I wouldn't do, conflicts began to arise at home—both with Cheryl and the kids.

It came to a head finally when we were living in the Tampa, Florida, area when my oldest daughter, Christy, was headed to the final four women's high school soccer state championship games in Miami. The challenge—they were on a Saturday and Sunday and I was a senior pastor.

"I can't be away from the church on Sunday, so I'll need to stay here." Cheryl looked at me and evenly said, "Then you'll be at the church alone, because I will be in Miami watching Christy in one of the most special and important times of her life."

The cold water had splashed all over my face. I must have been drenched from the wake-up call. And feeling like I was drenched from the splash in the face, I realized I was unintentionally repeating the same behavior that had wounded me as a teen. While the shock to my system was staggering, I found myself in Miami for the weekend celebrating a milestone in my daughter's life.

It would take me extended time to change this pattern of my life (and I still work on it). During the ensuing years, it would require some cross-country red-eye flights, long, exhausting drives, and adjusted schedules to get back for my kids' events, but it became a major priority—one that wasn't always even recognized, like the time I was given tickets to the Super Bowl and passed on them in order to be there to see my youngest daughter off to a dance.

But the fact remains: I made the right choice, and I stopped an unintentional generational passage in its tracks. And *that* feels good.

One other story. My adopted dad would never have asked me my opinion about a family decision when I was a teen. Kids were to "be seen and not heard." Decisions were for parents, not for kids. And with that happening repeatedly through my life, it is understandable how I took that perspective into my own family. So, we were living in Virginia and I was being invited to head a major North American ministry headquartered in Atlanta. I was struggling with the decision. Our oldest daughter was in college and our son was a junior in high school, while our youngest daughter in the seventh grade brought up the caboose of our clan.

As Cheryl and I labored over the pros and cons, the plusses and minuses, we struggled that a move would require travel and would fall between Bryan's junior and senior years. Remembering how I had been gone a lot, and through that had unintentionally left some Father Wounds, Cheryl suggested I talk to Bryan. She specifically said I should ask him if I took this role how much he felt I could be away from home overnight each month without it having an adverse impact on the family.

At first, I resisted (after all, my dad would never have done that!), but then I decided to give it a try. When I asked Bryan to come into the den and began to talk with him about a potential move, and then asked his opinion, he was probably as surprised that I was asking as I was to be doing the asking. He thought a few moments, and then said, "Dad, thanks for asking me my thoughts. May I have a couple of days to give it some thought and get back to you?"

By the time he approached me a few days later with, "Hey dad, I have an answer for you," I had forgotten what I asked. When he reminded me of our conversation, he continued with what would prove to be very wise words:

> *Dad, I think you could be gone seven to nine nights a month and we would be ok. But if you are gone more than that, something happens in our family. I don't know how to explain it. It's like when you are at home in your chair in the den and home at night, you don't even need to be doing homework with us or directly talking to us a lot. But we just see you in the chair and we know that everything is okay. But when you're gone a lot, everything changes. And everything isn't all right.*

A few years before, those words may have felt threatening. But that counsel proved to be extremely important to our future. I took the job in Atlanta, but I also worked hard with Cheryl to abide by our son's guidance. I hope it meant as much to Bryan to be heard, as it did for me to hear—and follow through. I'm sure I didn't meet the standard 100 percent of the time, but it was a great guide. I would even include Cheryl in the executive planning in my office monthly to help make sure I didn't step over the boundary we had set or repeat the wounds I had experienced as a teen.

And I'm still learning. Now it is with our grandkids. But I'm focusing overtime to do everything possible to not leave Father Wounds, or Grandfather Wounds, with the ones who mean so much to me.

It all comes down to *choices*. And often they're not easy. But making wise ones sure is important. I hope as you move through your future, you, too, will do everything in your power to leave plenty of Father Blessings and few—or better yet, *no*—Father Wounds!

NOTES

APPENDIX
SAMPLE LETTERS TO DAD

The following two letters were written by clients of mine (Dr. Rick Fowler) who wrote to their fathers concerning emotional wounds they encountered in their growing-up years. The purpose of sharing these letters is to provide a template for you when writing your letter to your dad. Over the many years I have been a licensed professional Christian counselor I have seen how the written word has spoken so powerfully and effectively to many fathers and step-fathers. I trust that first, these sample letters will be a helpful example and template for you as you write yours, and second, that your letter will also be fruitful as you write and share it.

Letter #1: A letter a professional NBA player wrote to his father:
Dear Dad,

Since I saw you, I have been doing a lot of thinking. I have been doing a psychological MRI on my life, my marriage, and my career. Ever since the note card and the conversation we had after Mary's wedding, I have realized I am not to blame. The events that took place that day after her wedding were the "straw that broke the camel's back."

First of all, I want to thank you for always providing for me, giving me a nice home to grow up in, and never letting me worry about making ends meet. I appreciate all that you did to take care of me and guide me growing up. I also wanted to thank you for giving me every opportunity to be successful in basketball.

I have always had a difficult time expressing my feelings, especially toward you. I have had a fear of showing my emotions since you made me feel like I was an "emotional wreck" whenever

I did make a mistake. You apparently thought mental toughness was a necessity in this basketball mind of yours, but what you forgot to consider was the boy you were raising, a person with feelings and needs, a human being. Life is not just about basketball; which I know you don't understand. I wish you would treat me like a person, not a basketball player. I was never allowed to think for myself. You always made the decisions for me and I had no independence.

As I write this letter, my mind is flooded with emotional puss wounds I have not been able to lance, such as:

1. I was never allowed to have a life with my peers outside of basketball.
2. I wasn't allowed to decide what major to focus on in college.
3. When around you, even as an adult today, you treat me like I am 10 years old.
4. You were so concerned I would lose focus on basketball that you would not let me date in high school.
5. Growing up, I was not allowed to attend a sleep over. I felt socially isolated because you only focused on basketball. You lived your life through me.
6. I do have anger issues. This trait is a result of pent-up emotions that I could not express as a child.
7. I have never heard you say that you were sorry for anything.
8. If I did not understand my English homework, I got hit in the head, and you cussed me out.
9. Even now you say I don't live up to my potential.
10. Most dads would be proud of their son's accomplishments, but not you. In your mind, I never will live up to my potential.
11. Your love for me was conditional based on my ability to perform on the court.

Dad, I am now an adult, an equal with you. So, from now on, for you to have a relationship with me, the following boundaries will have to be in place:

1. You must see my wife and me as equals. If you dishonor either of us, you will not be welcomed in our home.
2. If I want advice from you, I will ask for it. Otherwise I do not want you to comment at all about what I should do differently on the court.
3. I do not want you to attend any of my games until I feel I can sense that you love me for me and not for my performance.
4. I want you to list on paper, and send it to me, a list of wrongs you inflicted on me in my growing up years.
5. I also want you to write down, and send it to me, how you see our relationship moving forward if you are to see us as equals.

Right now, I am angry with you. However, for my kid's sake, I am willing to try. Reestablishing a relationship with you will take time, and when I am convinced that you have changed, then at that time we can talk about how we can form a positive connection moving forward. Our negative relationship has affected all areas of my life (including my marriage and floor performance), and I will no longer let you be the reason for that.

The choice is yours, Dad. Will you continue to be your old self, or will you humble yourself? Let me know what your decision is.

Yours Truly,

Xxxxxxxxxx

Letter #2: Son to his father: (Son, age 22)

Dad, I have been going to counseling in order to see how my reactions to daily life are affected by the "tapes" I keep playing in my head. My counselor has helped me realize why I tend to sabotage relationships when I feel I am getting emotionally attached.

I have written positives and negatives about my childhood and about each family member, trying to figure out why I feel insecure, jealous, and unsure of myself and my abilities.

Dad, as I wrote down the positives about you, I concluded that you are a wonderful, selfless provider. You have worked in a job you did not enjoy in order to support us. You went to all my school and college activities. You taught me to have a backbone, and to stand up for my beliefs.

As I was asked to think of the negative feelings I have about you, a major void surfaced—a void I have repressed for many years. That void was the fact that I have never felt an emotional closeness to you. Dad, I may be wrong about this, however it is the way I feel and if I am wrong, please help me understand why I feel this way.

Let me share some reasons why I believe there is this void with the hopes that you and I can regain what is missing and be able to establish healthy relationships with people outside of our family.

Observations I remember that are very real to me:

1. I feel your love for me is conditional. I feel I must fulfill your every wish to feel accepted. I don't feel I can make a decision if is against your better judgment.
2. You have personally blamed me for trying to ruin your marriage to mom.
3. I remember once you reached over the front seat of the car and hit me in the face when I asked you if I could drive.
4. Did it ever occur to you that you promised to take us on vacations, but you never did? Something always came up that caused you to cancel those trips.
5. In high school we all went to a concert and you blew up at me because I wanted to sit with some friends.

6. Dad, you never asked me what I want to do or what goals I have for my life.

As a result of therapy, I have recently become aware that my irresponsibility at times stems from my passive aggressive anger. I feel that my low self-image and my inability to trust my decisions are partly a result of my relationship with you.

Dad, it is very important for me to have a good relationship with you, yet in the future I want you to see me as an adult, not as a child. Please analyze what I have said for several days, and when I come home next weekend, I want to address our problem alone at Starbucks.

Until then,

xxxxxxxxx